"God has always wanted a people, but h[...] of growing confusion, Michael Reeves pr[...] identity in his book *Gospel People*. Captiv[...] truths that motivate and excite them, they [...] is not quick to judge and divide from others while contending for definitive doctrines that must be clearly proclaimed to a needy world."

Terry Virgo, Founder, Newfrontiers; author, *God's Treasured Possession*

"Michael Reeves has written a simple explanation of Christian faith. Reeves considers the word *evangelical* biblically, theologically, and historically. *Gospel People* is written in the best tradition of Ryle, Stott, and Packer yet reaches back to include the Puritans and the early church fathers as well. This book is simple, clear, and clarifying. Read and profit."

Mark Dever, Pastor, Capitol Hill Baptist Church, Washington, DC

"Michael Reeves is an evangelical in every best sense of the word—a gospel person who lives for the spiritual unity and integrity that his book *Gospel People* so beautifully illustrates. In a time of moral confusion, political polarization, and doctrinal apathy, Reeves gives the church a clear picture of Christian orthodoxy and the humble, holy lives that ordinary Christians ought to live as a result."

Philip Graham Ryken, President, Wheaton College

"In both contemporary culture and the contemporary church, the term *evangelical* is discussed, distorted, or debased to such an extent that some think it should be discarded. In *Gospel People*, Michael Reeves undertakes an engaging process of theological retrieval and provides a clear, concise, and compelling definition of *evangelicalism*. His approach is thoroughly grounded in Scripture and draws on the wisdom of church history down through the centuries. His focus on God's work of revelation, redemption, and regeneration will not only inform the mind but also warm the heart. His warnings against both doctrinal compromise and an overemphasis on secondary or tertiary issues will foster a deeper commitment to gospel unity and meaningful fellowship that is not rooted in mere politics or personalities."

John Stevens, National Director, Fellowship of Independent Evangelical Churches

"In *Gospel People*, Michael Reeves challenges us as evangelicals to take a fresh look at the foundation that is already laid, which is Jesus Christ as he is revealed by the Father in Scripture and in the power of the Spirit (1 Cor. 3:11). We are exhorted to build high together from that foundation for the glory of God. Anchored deeply in church history, this book is very convicting. It calls us to reexamine what we today may be wrongly holding up as the dividing line between friend and foe. May we heed its call!"

Conrad Mbewe, Pastor, Kabwata Baptist Church, Lusaka, Zambia

Gospel People

Other Crossway Books by Michael Reeves

Rejoice and Tremble: The Surprising Good News of the Fear of the Lord

Spurgeon on the Christian Life: Alive in Christ

Theologians You Should Know: An Introduction: From the Apostolic Fathers to the 21st Century

What Does It Mean to Fear the Lord?

Why the Reformation Still Matters, with Tim Chester

Gospel People

A Call for Evangelical Integrity

Michael Reeves

WHEATON, ILLINOIS

Library of Congress Cataloging-in-Publication Data

Names: Reeves, Michael (Michael Richard Ewert), author.
Title: Gospel people : a call for evangelical integrity / Michael Reeves.
Description: Wheaton, Illinois : Crossway, 2022. | Includes bibliographical references and index.
Identifiers: LCCN 2021029106 (print) | LCCN 2021029107 (ebook) | ISBN 9781433572937 (trade paperback) | ISBN 9781433572944 (pdf) | ISBN 9781433572951 (mobipocket) | ISBN 9781433572968 (epub)
Subjects: LCSH: Evangelicalism. | Evangelistic work.
Classification: LCC BR1640 .R438 2022 (print) | LCC BR1640 (ebook) | DDC 270.8/2—dc23
LC record available at https://lccn.loc.gov/2021029106
LC ebook record available at https://lccn.loc.gov/2021029107

How good and pleasant it is when brothers strive side by side for the faith of the gospel.

For Dan

Contents

Acknowledgments

THIS BOOK WOULD NOT BE what it is without the following people:

Dane Ortlund, who embodies what it means to be a person of the gospel, gave me the necessary push to put pen to paper.

Justin Taylor at Crossway generously went above and beyond what it means to be an editor and served as an exceptionally wise friend and counselor as I wrote.

Collin Hansen, Andrew Atherstone, Peter Comont, Dustin Benge, and John Stevens all read my initial manuscript and made many helpful comments that shaped the final work.

The team at Union, especially Joel Morris and Daniel Hames, supported and encouraged me as I wrote, modeling evangelical brotherliness and concern for the gospel.

My dear, wonderful wife, Bethan, who bore it all with me and upheld me with prayer and cheer.

To you all: thank you!

1

What Are Gospel People?

Beloved, although I was very eager to write to you
about our common salvation, I found it necessary
to write appealing to you to contend for the faith
that was once for all delivered to the saints.

JUDE 3

THIS IS A BOOK ABOUT being people of the gospel. In other words, this is a book about what it means to be evangelical. I believe that there is a *biblical* case to be made for the importance and the goodness of being evangelical.

I do not at all mean to defend everything that calls itself evangelical. Far from it. Looking around at the phenomenon of evangelicalism today, it often seems a mile wide and an inch deep. As Mark Noll famously put it, "The scandal of the evangelical mind is that there is not much of an evangelical mind."[1] The success of the label in the twentieth century meant that more and more wanted to appropriate it in some way, leaving it ever more theologically vacuous. Across the world, swathes have come to self-identify as evangelical without holding to classic evangelical beliefs. And then there is the problem of how being "evangelical" has become associated with particular cultures, with politics, or with race.

In other words, evangelicalism today is facing a crisis of integrity. "The evangelicals" are being defined—and even defining themselves—by agendas other than the gospel. We need to go back to our foundation, to "the faith that was once for all delivered to the saints," to become truly people *of the gospel*.

So what should it mean to be evangelical? We cannot simply look around at what we see of "evangelicalism" today. To understand and define evangelicalism properly, we must do as evangelicals themselves have traditionally done and hold it to its etymology in the evangel. Evangelicalism is defined by the evangel (*euangelion* being the Greek word for "good news"). Evangelicals are "gospel people," or people of the evangel. Some gospel people may dislike "evangelicalism," and others may use the label without being people of the gospel. But it is a distortion of the very meaning of the word "evangelical" to define it in any other way. To be evangelical, by definition, is not to be of a race or of a party, but of the gospel.

Evangelicalism, then, must be defined *theologically*. To be evangelical means to act, not out of cultural or political leanings, but out of theological, biblical convictions. The subject matter of

---

[1]   Mark A. Noll, *The Scandal of the Evangelical Mind* (Grand Rapids, MI: Eerdmans, 1994), 3.

evangelicalism is the gospel, which is known through Scripture. Or, to put it more technically, its material principle is the gospel, and its formal principle is the truth and supremacy of the Scriptures where that gospel is found. It is a commitment to the good news of Jesus Christ found in Scripture. It is uneccentric Christianity. That means that people of the gospel are evangelical, whether or not they choose to own the label. It also means that if something or someone purports to be evangelical, or is paraded in the media as such, and yet is not about the gospel, they are not evangelical. Whatever else they stand for is not proof of the emptiness or shapelessness of evangelicalism, but only that the label is no longer being applied accurately.

Evangelical Theology

There is no single, formal evangelical confession of faith one can sign. So is there such a thing as evangelical theology? We have seen so far that, by definition, the subject matter or material principle of evangelicalism must be the gospel. And it follows that its formal principle (or the way that subject matter is known) must be the truth and supremacy of the Scriptures where that gospel is found. But can we say more without promoting some party agenda? Let us see how the apostle Paul speaks of the gospel. Take, for example, the opening lines of his letter to the Romans:

> Paul, a servant of Christ Jesus, called to be an apostle, set apart for the gospel of God, which he promised beforehand through his prophets in the holy Scriptures, concerning his Son, who was descended from David according to the flesh and was declared to be the Son of God in power according to the Spirit

of holiness by his resurrection from the dead, Jesus Christ our Lord. (Rom. 1:1–4)

For Paul, the gospel is:

1. Trinitarian: it is the good news of the Father concerning his Son, who was declared the Son of God in power according to the Spirit.
2. Biblical: it is proclaimed through the holy Scriptures.
3. Christ-centered: it concerns God's Son.
4. Spirit-effected: it is by the Spirit that the Son is revealed.

We see the same when Paul writes to the Corinthians:

For Christ did not send me to baptize but to preach the gospel, and not with words of eloquent wisdom, lest the cross of Christ be emptied of its power.

For the word of the cross is folly to those who are perishing, but to us who are being saved it is the power of God. For it is written,

"I will destroy the wisdom of the wise,
and the discernment of the discerning I will thwart."

Where is the one who is wise? Where is the scribe? Where is the debater of this age? Has not God made foolish the wisdom of the world? For since, in the wisdom of God, the world did not know God through wisdom, it pleased God through the folly of what we preach to save those who believe. For Jews demand signs and Greeks seek wisdom, but we preach Christ crucified. . . .

And I, when I came to you, brothers, did not come proclaiming to you the testimony of God with lofty speech or wisdom. For I decided to know nothing among you except Jesus Christ and him crucified. And I was with you in weakness and in fear and much trembling, and my speech and my message were not in plausible words of wisdom, but in demonstration of the Spirit and of power, so that your faith might not rest in the wisdom of men but in the power of God. (1 Cor. 1:17–23; 2:1–5)

Again, Paul is clear that the gospel:

1. is not human wisdom but God the Father's revealed wisdom;
2. concerns Jesus Christ and him crucified; and
3. is made effective in the power of the Spirit.

And later in 1 Corinthians, the apostle returns to consider the matters "of first importance" with similar emphases:

Now I would remind you, brothers, of the gospel I preached to you, which you received, in which you stand, and by which you are being saved, if you hold fast to the word I preached to you—unless you believed in vain.

For I delivered to you as of first importance what I also received: that Christ died for our sins in accordance with the Scriptures, that he was buried, that he was raised on the third day in accordance with the Scriptures. (1 Cor. 15:1–4)

As before, the gospel is described by Paul as:

1. Biblical: it is in accordance with the Scriptures.
2. Christ-centered: it concerns Christ and his redemptive work, especially his death and resurrection.
3. Regenerative: though the Spirit is not expressly mentioned, the gospel is spoken of not as mere information, but as a message of personal salvation.

I will give just one more example, from Paul's letter to the Galatians. Writing to defend the gospel to a people who "are turning to a different gospel" (1:6), he says, first of all,

> I would have you know, brothers, that the gospel that was preached by me is not man's gospel. For I did not receive it from any man, nor was I taught it, but I received it through a revelation of Jesus Christ. (1:11–12)

He then emphatically concludes,

> See with what large letters I am writing to you with my own hand. It is those who want to make a good showing in the flesh who would force you to be circumcised, and only in order that they may not be persecuted for the cross of Christ. For even those who are circumcised do not themselves keep the law, but they desire to have you circumcised that they may boast in your flesh. But far be it from me to boast except in the cross of our Lord Jesus Christ, by which the world has been crucified to me, and I to the world. For neither circumcision counts for anything, nor uncircumcision, but a new creation. (6:11–15)

As in his letters to the Romans and Corinthians, Paul here speaks of the gospel as:

1. Revelation: it is not man's gospel, but one revealed by God.
2. Redemption: it concerns the cross of our Lord Jesus Christ.
3. Regeneration: it brings the radical renewal of a new creation.

Any definition of the evangel and so of evangelicalism must follow apostolic teaching with its essential qualities of being Trinitarian, Scripture-based, Christ-centered, and Spirit-renewed. It must therefore be God-centered as the "gospel of God" (Rom. 1:1), concerning the Father, the Son, and the Spirit and the work of the Father, the Son, and the Spirit. And to be faithful to the apostolic gospel, it must share Paul's concern for each of those indispensable three r's: *revelation*, *redemption*, and *regeneration*.

In that light, I suggest that true evangelicalism has a clear theology, and that at its heart lie three essential heads of doctrine, out of which flow all its concerns:

1. The Father's revelation in the Bible
2. The Son's redemption in the gospel
3. The Spirit's regeneration of our hearts[2]

These serve as a simple "table of contents" of evangelicalism. It is worth noting that this outline follows the shape of both the Nicene Creed and the Apostles' Creed, demonstrating that

---

2 See John Stott, *Evangelical Truth: A Personal Plea for Unity* (Leicester: IVP, 1999), 28, 103; and J. I. Packer, *The Evangelical Anglican Identity Problem: An Analysis* (Oxford: Latimer House, 1978), 20–23.

evangelicalism seeks not only to be plain, biblical Christianity, but creedal, catholic Christianity.

It is but an outline. My aim over the next three chapters is to unpack an evangelical, biblical understanding of those doctrines, summarized in this diagram:

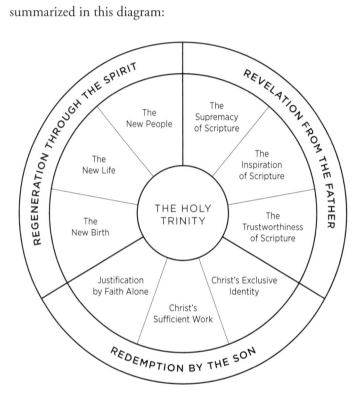

Then, when we have seen the defining theology of evangelicalism, we will be in a position to see how Paul's letter to the Romans gives an argument for the importance of evangelicalism.

"Evangelicalism" will be a threadbare, washed-up cultural relic for as long as it stands on any other foundation than this apostolic gospel. But where people of the gospel have integrity to this gospel, we will see something of heavenly beauty and fruitfulness: a heartfelt unity in, and striving together for, the faith once and for all delivered to the saints.

2

Revelation from the Father

"THE FIRST LEADING FEATURE in Evangelical Religion," wrote J. C. Ryle, "is the *absolute supremacy it assigns to Holy Scripture*, as the only rule of faith and practice, the only test of truth, the only judge of controversy."[1] Why so? Quite simply, because that is what Jesus taught about how we can know the truth.

The Supremacy of Scripture

Here is Mark's account of Jesus's controversy with the Pharisees over Scripture and its authority:

> Now when the Pharisees gathered to him, with some of the scribes who had come from Jerusalem, they saw that some of his disciples ate with hands that were defiled, that is, unwashed. (For the Pharisees and all the Jews do not eat unless they wash their hands properly, holding to the tradition of the elders, and

---

1   J. C. Ryle, *Knots Untied* (London: Chas. J. Thynne, 1900), 3.

when they come from the marketplace, they do not eat unless they wash. And there are many other traditions that they observe, such as the washing of cups and pots and copper vessels and dining couches.) And the Pharisees and the scribes asked him, "Why do your disciples not walk according to the tradition of the elders, but eat with defiled hands?" And he said to them, "Well did Isaiah prophesy of you hypocrites, as it is written,

"'This people honors me with their lips,
    but their heart is far from me;
in vain do they worship me,
    teaching as doctrines the commandments of men.'

You leave the commandment of God and hold to the tradition of men."

And he said to them, "You have a fine way of rejecting the commandment of God in order to establish your tradition! For Moses said, 'Honor your father and your mother'; and, 'Whoever reviles father or mother must surely die.' But you say, 'If a man tells his father or his mother, "Whatever you would have gained from me is Corban"' (that is, given to God)—then you no longer permit him to do anything for his father or mother, thus making void the word of God by your tradition that you have handed down. And many such things you do." (Mark 7:1–13)

The dispute arose over a simple matter of handwashing. To be clear, this was not about personal hygiene. The Pharisees and scribes did not merely dislike grubby paws at the dinner table.

Their concern was a religious one, that they might be "defiled" (v. 2). They therefore insisted on a ceremonial handwashing, according "to the tradition of the elders" (v. 3). Their objection to Jesus was that his disciples did not walk according to this tradition (v. 5). To this, Jesus replied, "You leave the commandment of God and hold to the tradition of men" (v. 8). Clearly, for Jesus, whereas Scripture is *of God*, tradition is *of men*, and it is vain hypocrisy to equate "the commandments of men" with the "doctrines" of God (v. 7).

Next, Jesus goes on to elaborate on his view of Scripture and tradition by challenging the teaching of the Pharisees about Corban. "Corban" is a Hebrew word for a gift given to God, and evidently the tradition had grown up that when something had been intended as Corban, it could never then be used for anything else. Jesus imagines the case of a young man who has set aside some money as Corban, only then to find that his aged parents were in need. In that situation, Jesus argues, the Pharisees would "no longer permit him to do anything for his father or mother" (v. 12) because of that tradition concerning Corban. But in so doing, they would make the young man violate Moses's commands: "Honor your father and your mother" (Ex. 20:12) and "Whoever curses his father or his mother shall be put to death" (Ex. 21:17). Thus, they sinfully reject the word *of God* to uphold the tradition *of the elders*. In fact, by not permitting something that Scripture commanded, they had set themselves up over the word of God as higher authorities.

Jesus's conviction is plain: Scripture is divine in origin, even when Moses spoke the words. What "Moses said" (v. 10) is "the word of God" (v. 13). As such, Scripture's authority is supreme.

Any human reasoning or tradition (which is human in origin) is subordinate to Scripture, and we must reject any thinking or tradition that is in conflict with Scripture, and not vice versa. The word of God and the words of mere creatures are not and cannot be equal authorities. Thus, when the divine word conflicts with human words, it is Scripture that must be heeded and tradition that must be rejected. As Jesus demonstrated every time he asked, "Have you not read in the Scriptures?" or, "What is written in the Law?" he believed that Scripture is the supreme, sufficient authority that must overrule all our words and thoughts.

Again and again since the close of the New Testament, the church has reasserted this essential evangelical principle of the supremacy of Scripture alone. In the second century, Irenaeus put the supremacy of Scripture at the heart of his response to gnosticism. Scripture, he asserted, is "the ground and pillar of our faith."[2] The prime mistake of the gnostics, he argued, was to read Scripture through nonscriptural principles, forcing it to fit into an alien mold. Scripture cannot be so read, according to Irenaeus; rather, Scripture can be understood only by Scripture. No other knowledge, theological system, or oral tradition can accurately mediate the true meaning of Scripture.[3] Nearly two centuries later, Athanasius wrote of the canonical books of Scripture: "These are fountains of salvation, that they who thirst may be satisfied with

---

2 Irenaeus, *Against Heresies*, 3.1.1, in *The Apostolic Fathers with Justin Martyr and Ire-naeus*, ed. Alexander Roberts, James Donaldson, and A. Cleveland Coxe, vol. 1 of *The Ante-Nicene Fathers* (Buffalo, NY: Christian Literature Company, 1885), 414.

3 Irenaeus, *Against Heresies*, 3.12.9 (434). Irenaeus did value the direct connection between the apostles and the bishops in his day. However, that never served as a grid to force Scripture through, but as proof that the plain truth of Scripture had been preserved and not distorted by the church.

the living words they contain. In these alone is proclaimed the doctrine of godliness. Let no man add to these, neither let him take ought from these."[4] A generation later, Gregory of Nyssa (c. 335–c. 395) would yet again articulate the same belief in the supremacy of Scripture:

> We do not think that it is right to make their prevailing custom the law and rule of sound doctrine. For if custom is to avail for proof of soundness, we too, surely, may advance our prevailing custom; and if they reject this, we are surely not bound to follow theirs. Let the inspired Scripture, then, be our umpire, and the vote of truth will surely be given to those whose dogmas are found to agree with the Divine words.[5]

And another generation after that, Augustine would write, "For the reasonings of any men whatsoever, even though they be Catholics, and of high reputation, are not to be treated by us in the same way as the canonical Scriptures are treated."[6]

---

4   Athanasius, Letter 39 in *St. Athanasius: Select Works and Letters*, trans. Henry Burgess and Jessie Smith Payne, vol. 4 of *A Select Library of the Nicene and Post-Nicene Fathers of the Christian Church*, 2nd ser., ed. Philip Schaff and Henry Wace (New York: Christian Literature Company, 1892), 552.

5   Gregory of Nyssa, "On the Holy Trinity, and of the Godhead of the Holy Spirit," in *Gregory of Nyssa: Dogmatic Treatises, Etc.*, trans. Henry Austin Wilson, vol. 5 of *A Select Library of the Nicene and Post-Nicene Fathers of the Christian Church*, 2nd ser., ed. Philip Schaff and Henry Wace (New York: Christian Literature Company, 1893), 327.

6   To be clear, for Augustine "Catholic" means the opposite of heterodox, not the opposite of Protestant. Augustine, Letter 148.15 in *The Confessions and Letters of St. Augustin with a Sketch of His Life and Work*, trans. J. G. Cunningham, vol. 1 of *A Select Library of the Nicene and Post-Nicene Fathers of the Christian Church*, 1st ser., ed. Philip Schaff, (Buffalo, NY: Christian Literature Company, 1886), 502.

It was a millennium later, though, at the time of the Reformation, that the matter of the supremacy of Scripture would come into particularly sharp relief. It would do so because Martin Luther found himself challenging a church in Rome that *did* affirm Scripture's authority but did not believe that Scripture is the *supreme* authority. Rome's position was spelled out by Sylvester Prierias, the first theologian appointed by the pope to debate Luther: "He who does not accept the doctrine of the Church of Rome and pontiff of Rome as an infallible rule of faith, *from which the Holy Scriptures, too, draw their strength and authority*, is a heretic."[7] And still today, the *Catechism of the Catholic Church* teaches that "the Church, to whom the transmission and interpretation of Revelation is entrusted, does not derive her certainty about all revealed truths from the holy Scriptures alone. Both Scripture and Tradition must be accepted and honored with equal sentiments of devotion and reverence."[8]

However, the insistence of Luther's interlocutors on the authority of the pope only seemed to clarify the issue in the Reformer's mind. He came to see that if the Roman Catholic Church held the pope to be an authority equal to or even above Scripture, she could never be reformed by God's word. The pope's word would always trump God's. Luther became increasingly clear that the pope was abusing Scripture, and that a man could never be an authority higher than God's word. Any man who puts himself above God's word is putting himself in the place of God. After

7   Quoted in Heiko A. Oberman, *Luther: Man Between God and the Devil* (New Haven, CT: Yale University Press, 1982), 193; emphasis added.

8   Catholic Church, *Catechism of the Catholic Church*, par. 82, Vatican (website), accessed July 20, 2021, https://www.vatican.va/content/vatican/en.html.

all, the church has not brought the word of God into being; it is God's word that has brought the church into being, just as God's word first brought creation into being. God's word comes first.

In fact, without this principle of the supremacy of Scripture there would have been no Reformation. It is the first principle that distinguishes Luther (the first Reformer) from Erasmus, the scholar who made the Greek New Testament widely available, but who is never counted as a Reformer. Erasmus had a clear regard for Scripture, but he would never have used Scripture to bring about any serious reformation. For him, the Scriptures held no clear governing authority and so no ability to challenge and to change substantially. The Bible was not supreme for Erasmus, "and so its message could be tailored, squeezed and adjusted to fit his own vision of what Christianity was." To "achieve any substantial reformation, it took Luther's attitude, that Scripture is the only sure foundation for belief (*sola Scriptura*). The Bible had to be acknowledged as the supreme authority and allowed to contradict and overrule all other claims, or else it would itself be overruled and its message hijacked. In other words, a simple reverence for the Bible and acknowledgement that it has some authority would never have been enough to bring about the Reformation. *Sola Scriptura* was the indispensable key for change."[9]

We can get even clearer on what the supremacy of Scripture means if we compare two more men: Jonathan Edwards (1703–1758) and Friedrich Schleiermacher (1768–1834). Jonathan Edwards stood squarely in the evangelical tradition; Friedrich Schleiermacher is known as the father of liberal theology. Yet

9   Michael Reeves, *The Unquenchable Flame: Discovering the Heart of the Reformation* (Nashville, TN: B&H Academic, 2010), 189.

there were some similarities: close in time, they both faced the challenge of the Enlightenment and agreed that true faith is more than assent to a list of doctrines. Both emphasized the importance of experience and religious affections. But otherwise they came from different theological universes. When Edwards wrote about a believer's affections, he explained, "Holy affections are not heat without light; but evermore arise from some information of the understanding, some spiritual instruction that the mind receives, some light or actual knowledge."[10] In other words, the heat of our affections—our delight in God and our love for him—come from the light of God's truth. God's word affects us. For Schleiermacher, however, it was the other way around. "Christian doctrines," he wrote, "are accounts of the Christian religious affections set forth in speech."[11] That is, for Schleiermacher, Christian doctrines are nothing more than the product of our religious affections. God's word has not produced those affections; our feelings have produced our beliefs. Our faith is based on what we feel. That idea would set the trajectory for liberal theology by making human feelings and human reason supreme over Scripture.

Scripture and Other Authorities

From this quick historical survey, we can see the basic difference between the evangelical approach to Scripture and the main al-

---

10 Jonathan Edwards, *Religious Affections*, in *The Works of Jonathan Edwards*, vol. 2, ed. John E. Smith (New Haven, CT: Yale University Press, 2009), 266.

11 Friedrich Schleiermacher, *The Christian Faith* (2nd ed. of *Der Christliche Glaube*, 1830–1831), ed. H. R. Mackintosh and J. S. Stewart (Edinburgh: T&T Clark, 1999), §15 (76).

ternatives. Roman Catholicism looks to Scripture and tradition together as equal authorities (much as in Eastern Orthodoxy). Liberal theologians in the tradition of Schleiermacher see human reason and feeling as their primary guiding light. In contrast with both, the evangelical approach follows Jesus's teaching that Scripture is the word of God and must therefore overrule all the words and thoughts and feelings and traditions of men. And to be clear, it is not simply that evangelicals have a high regard for Scripture. The Pharisees had that much. To be evangelical means to stand with Christ against the Pharisees in submitting to Scripture as *supreme* in its authority and so refusing to make "void the word of God" (Mark 7:13) by our own traditions, thoughts or feelings. To be evangelical means Scripture trumps all.

Of course, not everything that has called itself evangelical has held to this evangelical principle, and not always has this principle been well understood. Too often, self-confessed evangelicals have veered toward an anti-intellectual "me and my Bible" biblicism that rejects *all* wisdom found elsewhere. But *sola Scriptura* is not the same as the view that we should have "no creed but the Bible!" That is a subevangelical position. Jesus did not reject all human traditions out of hand, but would celebrate the Feast of Dedication and recline at table to eat, according to the custom of the day. The apostle Paul, who taught that even the apparent foolishness of God "is wiser than men" (1 Cor. 1:25), could also affirm that unbelievers could know and speak some truth. Addressing the philosophers of Athens, he quoted pagan poets who had managed to say something true, even though they had not properly comprehended that truth:

Yet he is actually not far from each one of us, for

"'In him we live and move and have our being';

as even some of your own poets have said,

"'For we are indeed his offspring.'

Being then God's offspring, we ought not to think that the divine being is like gold or silver or stone, an image formed by the art and imagination of man. (Acts 17:27–29)

Equally, the Reformers did not reject all tradition or insight from outside of Scripture. They wanted to renew the church, not invent a new one from scratch, and were eager to emphasize their continuity with the early church and so learn from it. For them, reforming involved retrieving. Thus, Luther would argue, church councils and creeds are good and important when they oppose error and maintain the faith. His only caveat was that

a council has no power *to establish new articles of faith*, even though the Holy Spirit is present. Even the apostolic council in Jerusalem introduced nothing new in matters of faith, but rather held that which St. Peter concludes in Acts 16 [15:11], and which all their predecessors believed, namely, the article that one is to be saved without the laws, solely through the grace of Christ.[12]

12 Martin Luther, *Church and Ministry III*, vol. 41 of *Luther's Works*, ed. Jaroslav Jan Pelikan, Hilton C. Oswald, and Helmut T. Lehmann (Philadelphia, PA: Fortress, 1999), 123.

And the confessions of faith that came out of the Reformation followed suit. For example, the Thirty-Nine Articles of Religion of the Anglican Communion states,

> The Church hath power to decree Rites or Ceremonies, and authority in Controversies of Faith: and yet it is not lawful for the Church to ordain any thing that is contrary to God's Word written, neither may it so expound one place of Scripture, that it be repugnant to another. Wherefore, although the Church be a witness and a keeper of Holy Writ, yet, as it ought not to decree any thing against the same, so besides the same ought it not to enforce any thing to be believed for necessity of Salvation.[13]

To be evangelical is to believe what the church as a whole has always taught. It is to be uneccentric. For the word of God has been given to the church as a whole, and while we do read it individually, even then we do so as part of the congregation. As such, we should want to hear the word expounded by trustworthy teachers, and to hear their insights; we should want to listen to the wisdom of the saints, both dead and alive.

Perhaps the main reason why evangelicals have sometimes been historically shortsighted and biblicist ("no creed but the Bible!") is the fear that some tradition or insight could become the *supreme* authority. It is a reasonable and right fear. We must see to it "that no one takes you captive by philosophy and empty deceit, according to human tradition, according to the elemental

13 Thirty Nine Articles of Religion, Article XX, Anglican Communion (website), accessed July 20, 2021, https://www.anglicancommunion.org/.

spirits of the world, and not according to Christ" (Col. 2:8). However, that carefulness must not become a panicked retreat from all learning or all tradition. Instead, we simply need to be clear that reason and tradition have a *ministerial* authority. It should therefore trouble us when we go against established Christian precedent. Such precedent, however, does not have a *magisterial* authority. Only Scripture does. Scripture is our bookshelf; tradition is the record of what the church has read or misread there; reason is the set of spectacles we wear as we seek to make sense of what we read.[14]

There are a number of authorities to which the healthy evangelical will want to submit: the governing authorities of the land (Rom. 13:1), church elders, and creeds. But none of those authorities, along with Christian tradition and reason, are infallibly trustworthy like the word of God. They are of men. Scripture is of God. They must bow to Scripture, not the other way around. They should be listened to, but Scripture must reign supreme. J. C. Ryle summed up the evangelical position well when he wrote,

> Evangelical Religion *does not despise learning*, research, or the wisdom of days gone by. It is not true to say that we do. In thorough appreciation of anything that throws light on God's Word, we give place to none. Let any one look over the lists of those who in days gone by have been eminent for theological scholarship in this country, and I am bold to say he will find some of the most eminent are Evangelical men. . . . But while

---

14 I am indebted to N. T. Wright for this image. Taken from *The Last Word: Scripture and the Authority of God—Getting Beyond the Bible Wars* (San Francisco, CA: HarperOne, 2006), 101.

we do not despise learning, we steadily refuse to place any uninspired writings on a level with revelation.[15]

The Inspiration of Scripture

The reason why evangelicals treat Scripture as their supreme authority is because it is the word *of God*. In other words, evangelicals believe in what is traditionally called the "inspiration" of Scripture. Today, the word *inspiration* can be a little misleading, as if Moses, Paul, and Luke simply felt enthused one day and started scribbling. That is not at all what is meant! By *inspiration* is meant what Paul teaches Timothy when he writes of how

> from childhood you have been acquainted with the sacred writings, which are able to make you wise for salvation through faith in Christ Jesus. All Scripture is breathed out by God and profitable for teaching, for reproof, for correction, and for training in righteousness, that the man of God may be complete, equipped for every good work. (2 Tim. 3:15–17)

That is, all the "writings" of all of Scripture are "breathed out by God." They are exhaled by God. In a sense, to capture Paul's meaning here, it might be more accurate (if a little odd-sounding) to speak of the *ex-piration* rather than the *in-spiration* of Scripture. But that is his meaning. It is not merely some parts of Scripture that are God-breathed; it is not merely the big ideas of Scripture: all of it, in every part and in every word, is God-breathed. To capture this, theologians speak of the *plenary*

15 Ryle, *Knots Untied*, 9–10.

inspiration of Scripture to express the fact that the whole of Scripture is God-breathed, and *verbal* inspiration to be clear that every word of the original is included.

In order to read the word of God aright, evangelicals should be eager to recognize that Scripture presents itself as having dual authorship. Thus, Luke can write in the same passage interchangeably of "the Law of Moses" and "the Law of the Lord" (Luke 2:22–23). Occasionally, we see this means that God actually dictated his words, as at Sinai when "Moses wrote down all the words of the Lord" (Ex. 24:4). More normally it means that "men spoke from God as they were carried along by the Holy Spirit" (2 Pet. 1:21). That is, David, John, and Matthew themselves were writing, and writing in such a way that their own distinct personalities come through in the text. Yet they wrote "in the Holy Spirit" (Mark 12:36), "carried along" (2 Pet. 1:21) and guided in every word they wrote by the Holy Spirit. They were not inventing or just speaking their own opinions; they were different-sounding instruments, all played by the same divine musician. Thus, *every* word of Scripture—including every word of Hosea, Mark, and Jude—can be seen to be God-breathed.

The Total Trustworthiness of Scripture

This too is part and parcel of the evangelical principle of the supremacy of Scripture. Scripture can be our supreme authority only if it is entirely truthful and therefore totally trustworthy. If it was faulty, how could we allow it to overrule all else? But we can submit to it with confidence because of our Lord. Jesus was consistently clear that what Scripture says, God says. So, for example, in a conversation with the Pharisees about divorce, he said,

"Have you not read that he who created them from the beginning made them male and female, and said, 'Therefore a man shall leave his father and his mother and hold fast to his wife, and the two shall become one flesh'? So they are no longer two but one flesh. What therefore God has joined together, let not man separate." (Matt. 19:4–6)

Here, Jesus is quoting Genesis 2:24, which in context is not a statement attributed to God but a comment by the narrator. Yet Jesus sees these as the very words of "he who created them." For Jesus, Scripture is the word of God, and as such he could teach "Scripture cannot be broken" (John 10:35). To suggest that the word of God might be faulty or untrustworthy is to imply that God is faulty and untrustworthy. But he *is* truth, he is perfect, he is trustworthy, and so must his word be. The perfection of the word of God flows naturally from the perfection of God.

It has sometimes been suggested that because of Scripture's dual authorship—the fact that God speaks through his prophets and apostles—it does contain mistakes. After all, it is argued, to err is human. But that is simply not the case: Adam was not originally sinful, nor was the man Jesus, the one in whom we see sinless humanity as we should be. As God perfectly revealed himself through the humanity of Jesus, so he perfectly speaks through the human authors of Scripture. Otherwise Scripture could be broken. Evangelicals can therefore say with the apostle Paul, "Let God be true though every one were a liar" (Rom. 3:4). Every word of Scripture is breathed out by a trustworthy God, and we can therefore trust it as Jesus did. None of which is to say that anyone is *saved* by belief in the trustworthiness of Scripture.

You may be a *Christian* and still believe the Bible faulty, but it is not *evangelical* to say that Scripture is untrustworthy.

None of this is an eccentric, modern spin on mainstream Christianity. This is what Irenaeus taught in the second century: "the Scriptures are indeed perfect, since they were spoken by the Word of God and His Spirit."[16] And

> let us revert to the Scriptural proof furnished by those apostles who did also write the Gospel, in which they recorded the doctrine regarding God, pointing out that our Lord Jesus Christ is the truth, and that no lie is in Him. As also David says, prophesying His birth from a virgin, and the resurrection from the dead, "Truth has sprung out of the earth." The apostles, likewise, being disciples of the truth, are above all falsehood; for a lie has no fellowship with the truth, just as darkness has none with light, but the presence of the one shuts out that of the other.[17]

It is what Augustine taught: "I have learned," he wrote, "to yield this respect and honour only to the canonical books of Scripture: of these alone do I most firmly believe that the authors were completely free from error."[18] Indeed, he argued, "it seems to me that most disastrous consequences must follow upon our believing that anything false is found in the sacred books: that is to say, that the men by whom the Scripture has been given to us, and committed to writing, did put down in these books anything false."[19]

---

16 Irenaeus, *Against Heresies* 2.28.2 (399).
17 Irenaeus, *Against Heresies* 3.5.1 (417).
18 Augustine of Hippo, Letter 132.3 (350).
19 Augustine of Hippo, Letter 28.3 (251–52).

And it was precisely this that enabled Luther to distinguish between the respect he would pay to tradition and the complete submission he would yield only to Scripture:

> Since the fathers have often erred, as you yourself confess, who will make us certain as to wherein they have not erred, assuming their reputation is sufficient and should not be weighed and judged according to the divine Scriptures? They have (you say) also interpreted the Scriptures. What if they erred in their interpretation, as well as in their life and writings? In that way you make gods of all that is human in us, and of men themselves; and the word of men you make equal to the Word of God.[20]

In other words, the fathers are not infallibly trustworthy, and so cannot be heeded unconditionally. They are therefore not like the word of God.

Yet in the last century, following the lead of the Swiss theologian Karl Barth in particular, the charge has been made that this view is nothing but a bit of modernist rationalism. Barth called it a "new understanding of biblical inspiration."[21] His fear was that Protestant orthodoxy wanted to put the Bible in a box to bring it under human control. That way, rather than depending on the grace of God, we could become masters and lords of the word of God. A human doctrine would put the divine

---

20 Martin Luther, *Word and Sacrament II*, vol. 36 of *Luther's Works*, ed. Jaroslav Jan Pelikan, Hilton C. Oswald, and Helmut T. Lehmann (Philadelphia, PA: Fortress, 1999), 136.

21 Karl Barth, *Church Dogmatics* (Edinburgh: T&T Clark, 1956–1972), I/2, 522.

word on a leash. Or to put it another way, we have created the doctrine of Scripture's trustworthiness *so that* we might trust the word of God.

Those are serious charges, and if found guilty, we can no longer honestly call ourselves evangelical. If our allegiance to the word of God depends on some prior allegiance to a human doctrine, then we must come clean and admit we are as mistaken as the Pharisees. But that is absolutely not the evangelical intention. Evangelicals do not believe Scripture is trustworthy *because of* some doctrine of inspiration or inerrancy or infallibility. They believe it is trustworthy because Jesus teaches it and Scripture proves itself to be so. And as for any modernist rationalism in their thinking about the Bible, they want to repent of it wherever it can be shown unscriptural. As John Stott argued,

> What we evangelicals want to be is plain, Bible Christians. This is why our claiming that the evangelical faith is the historic Christian faith is not the arrogant claim it may sound, although it has sometimes been put forward in an arrogant way. If it can be shown that we have misunderstood or distorted the biblical message whether by addition or by subtraction, whether by manipulation or by deviation, then we must be ready and eager immediately to change. Our aim, in humility, is to be loyal to the biblical revelation.[22]

In that statement, Stott put his finger on an important reason why many object to the evangelical understanding of Scripture: it

---

22 Michael Reeves and John Stott, *The Reformation: What You Need to Know and Why* (Peabody, MA: Hendrickson, 2017), 31.

is because we still manage to misunderstand or distort the biblical message. But our failures to read Scripture aright say nothing about its actual trustworthiness; they only tell us that to have even the highest view of Scripture is not yet to be biblical. It is not our *reading* of Scripture that is totally trustworthy: we can hold the highest view of Scripture and use bad interpretation, bad harmonizing, bad apologetics, and bad theology.

It helps here to read the careful way in which the Chicago Statement on Biblical Inerrancy speaks:

> Holy Scripture, being God's own Word, written by men prepared and superintended by His Spirit, is of infallible divine authority in all matters upon which it touches: it is to be believed, as God's instruction, in all that it affirms; obeyed, as God's command, in all that it requires; embraced, as God's pledge, in all that it promises.[23]

It is to be believed *in all that it affirms*.[24] So a belief in the complete trustworthiness of Scripture does not mean, for example, that we can read Psalm 14:1 out of context and hold that "there is no God." We must read it with sensitivity to context, interpreting Scripture by Scripture and not allowing our reading of a passage to contradict what Scripture plainly teaches elsewhere. We must

---

23 "The Chicago Statement on Biblical Inerrancy," Short Statement 2, The Evangelical Theological Society (website), accessed July 20, 2021, https://www.etsjets.org/files/documents/Chicago_Statement.pdf.

24 The Lausanne Covenant speaks the same language, describing Scripture as "without error in all that it affirms." John Stott, ed., *Making Christ Known: Historic Mission Documents from the Lausanne Movement 1974–1989* (Milton Keynes: Paternoster, 1997), 13–14.

read it with sensitivity to genre. History must be read as history, poetry as poetry, and so on.

But with that caution in place, evangelicals can gladly affirm that Scripture is not just true and trustworthy in its overall purpose or when it speaks of spiritual matters. It is of "infallible divine authority in *all* matters upon which it touches." It is the word of God in full and in every part. Thus, evangelicals seek to teach and uphold *all* that Scripture teaches, and with the clarity, weighting, and urgency that Scripture gives each matter.

The old tempter will always whisper, "Did God actually say?" But if evangelicals do not hold this first principle, that God's word rules us because it is his entirely truthful and therefore totally trustworthy word, then we will cease to be evangelical, whatever we call ourselves. Thus did B. B. Warfield warn:

> No wonder we are told that the same advance in knowledge which requires a changed view of the Bible necessitates also a whole new theology. If the New Testament writers are not trustworthy as teachers of doctrine and we have to go elsewhere for the source and norm of truth as to God and duty and immortality, it will not be strange if a very different system of doctrine from that delivered by the Scriptures and docilely received from them by the Church, results.[25]

To be clear, it is not that authentic evangelicalism depends simply upon our articulation of some impeccable formula about the Bible. All too easily, we can hold our beliefs in the ether and

---

25 B. B. Warfield, *Revelation and Inspiration*, vol. 1 of *The Works of Benjamin B. Warfield* (Grand Rapids, MI: Baker, 2003), 180.

not act on them. Authentic evangelicalism depends upon our submission to God's word as our supreme authority. Where God has spoken, we obey.

Do Evangelicals Worship the Bible?

Sometimes the charge is made that with such a high view of Scripture, evangelicals fall into bibliolatry, the worship of the Bible. Naturally, evangelicals tend to be quick to deny this, but there can actually be something to it. As Bernard Ramm wrote, "The temptation of biblicism is that it can speak of the inspiration of the Scriptures *apart from* the Lord they enshrine."[26] That is, we can commit the sin of the Pharisees, diligently studying the Scriptures because we think that in them we have eternal life, yet failing to come to Christ, the one to whom they bear witness (John 5:39–40). Such biblicism, by definition, cannot be truly *evangelical*, for it ignores the evangel.

The problem, though, is not the high view of Scripture, which Jesus himself had; it is thinking that life is to be had in the Scriptures *by themselves*, as if mere understanding of them equals saving faith. Such a view is not scriptural and therefore not truly evangelical. The Scriptures do not point to themselves: they "are able to make you wise for salvation *through faith in Christ Jesus*" (2 Tim. 3:15). They are God the Father's revelation of the Son through the Spirit. As J. I. Packer put it,

Holy Scripture should be thought of as *God preaching*—God preaching to me every time I read or hear any part of it—God

26 Bernard Ramm, *Special Revelation and the Word of God* (Grand Rapids, MI: Eerdmans, 1961), 117.

the Father preaching God the Son in the power of God the Holy Ghost. God the Father is the giver of Holy Scripture; God the Son is the theme of Holy Scripture; and God the Spirit, as the Father's appointed agent in witnessing to the Son, is the author, authenticator, and interpreter, of Holy Scripture.[27]

Evangelicals therefore stand unflinchingly under Scripture, but that stand should not make us legalists, pedants, or bibliolaters. For, as it was for Jesus himself, Scripture is not our end or objective: God is. The Spirit-breathed Scriptures bear witness to Christ, the living Word of the Father, that we may come to him and have life. Thus, the first principle of evangelicalism—the supremacy of Scripture—does not stand alone. It must lead on to the second.

---

27 J. I. Packer, *God Has Spoken: Revelation and the Bible*, 2nd ed. (London: Hodder and Stoughton, 1979), 97.

3

Redemption by the Son

THE EVANGEL OF GOD is news "concerning his Son" (Rom. 1:3), which is why the apostle Paul decided to know nothing among the Corinthians "except Jesus Christ and him crucified" (1 Cor. 2:2). To be faithful to the gospel means treating Christ and his redeeming death and resurrection as matters "of first importance" (1 Cor. 15:3–4). "The heartbeat of the gospel message," writes Conrad Mbewe, "is Christ's life, death, burial, and resurrection on our behalf. Once we lose this message, we have lost the means by which God will add to his church on earth real citizens of his kingdom."[1]

None of which may sound very surprising. Isn't such Christ-centeredness mere Christianity? Indeed it is, and yet through the centuries, Christians have kept managing to downgrade Jesus, cast him in their own image, or use him as the icing to sell some other agenda. It was said, for example, of the liberal theologian

1 Conrad Mbewe, *God's Design for the Church: A Guide for African Pastors and Ministry Leaders* (Wheaton, IL: Crossway, 2020), 62.

Adolf von Harnack that the "Christ that Harnack sees, looking back through nineteen centuries of Catholic darkness, is only the reflection of a Liberal Protestant face, seen at the bottom of a deep well."[2]

That is not the evangelical way. Evangelicals look to Scripture to know Christ, and there they find the unique Son of God, exclusive in his glorious identity and completely sufficient as a savior. Thus, wrote J. C. Ryle, another

> leading feature of Evangelical Religion is the paramount impor-
> tance it attaches to the work and office of our Lord Jesus Christ,
> and to the nature of the salvation which He has wrought out
> for man. Its theory is that the eternal Son of God, Jesus Christ,
> has by His life, death, and resurrection, as our Representative
> and Substitute, obtained a complete salvation for sinners, and
> a redemption from the guilt, power, and consequences of sin,
> and that all who believe on Him are, even while they live,
> completely forgiven and justified from all things, are reckoned
> completely righteous before God, are interested in Christ and
> all His benefits.[3]

The Exclusive Identity of Christ

The Gospel of John opens like a parting of the clouds with the most glorious possible assertion of the unique identity of Christ:

> In the beginning was the Word, and the Word was with God,
> and the Word was God. He was in the beginning with God.

---

2   George Tyrrell, *Christianity at the Crossroads* (London: Longmans, Green, 1909), 44.
3   J. C. Ryle, *Knots Untied* (London: Chas. J. Thynne, 1900), 5.

All things were made through him, and without him was not any thing made that was made. In him was life, and the life was the light of men. (John 1:1–4)

The one who would take flesh (v. 14) was the Word spoken out by the Father in his work of creation in Genesis 1. He is the expression of the Father through whom all things were created. He himself is not created: before things were made through him, he was with God and he was God. This Word of God is the one who belongs in the deepest, most essential closeness and oneness with God, and the one who displays the innermost reality of God's being. He is, as Hebrews 1:3 phrases it, "the radiance of the glory of God and the exact imprint of his nature." As such, "life" is not something to which he merely points the way, like some human prophet. He is the living one. He is life, and life is to be found "in him" (v. 4).

These truths about the Son of God are so vital they were the subject of what was perhaps the greatest battle the church fought in the centuries after the New Testament. As the words of the Nicene Creed show, Christians saw that the gospel depends upon Jesus Christ being "God from God, light from light, true God from true God, begotten not made, of one being with the Father." It means that there is no God in heaven who is unlike Jesus. And it means that he is, exclusively, the way, and the truth, and the life. No one can come to the Father except through him (John 14:6).

It is that eternal title of Christ's, "the Word of God," that John focuses on in the first few verses of his gospel. From verse 12, however, his emphasis shifts to another eternal title. In verse 12, it is only really a hint, as he writes of how "to all who did receive him, who believed in his name, he gave the right to become children of God." But what sort of being could give that blessing of adoption? Only one who is "the only Son from the Father, full of grace and truth" (v. 14). Only "the only God, who is at the Father's side" (v. 18). No other god could offer such a blessing apart from the one who is at the Father's side (or, more literally, "in the bosom of the Father"). When the Son takes his beloved one into his bosom (13:23), he brings them with him where he is (17:24): in the bosom of the Father.

John has thus affirmed for Christ an identity shared by no human teacher or savior-figure in any other belief system in the world. And on that identity the gospel stands. For if there is no eternal Son, God is not really a Father, and he could never give us the right to be his children. If Christ does not have this unique identity, he does not have the ability to bring us into the bosom of the Father. A mere creature could never share with us what he himself had never known.

John has also shown why Christ-centeredness is not imbalanced, as though such devotion to Christ disregards the Father and the Spirit. Christ's very identity is the Word who reveals God, and the Son beloved of the Father, and the Spirit-anointed one (or "Christ"). Thus, John issues a Trinitarian call to faith in Jesus: "but these are written so that you may believe that Jesus is the Christ, the Son of God, and that by believing you may have life in his name" (20:31). It means that for Christians to say with Paul "for me to live is Christ" (Phil. 1:21) is to share the Father's love and concern. To put Christ at the center of our theology is to do like the Father, who has his Son at the center of his "purpose, which he set forth in Christ as a plan for the fullness of time, to unite all things in him, things in heaven and things on earth" (Eph. 1:9–10). To bear witness to Christ is to keep in step with the Spirit (John 15:26–27), who inspired the biblical writers for that very purpose (5:46). "Christ alone stands at the center of God's eternal purposes, Christ alone is the object of our saving faith, and therefore Christ alone must stand at the very center of our theology."[4]

This evangelical principle of the exclusive identity of Christ has remained the backbone of how the church has thought of the gospel down the centuries. It fueled the early church's assertion of the uniqueness of Christ in the face of Roman pluralistic paganism. And it was pivotal to the argument of the church's first full-scale work of systematic theology, Irenaeus's *Against Heresies*. Irenaeus, using Paul's Adam-Christ typology (Rom. 5:12–21; 1 Cor. 15:20–23, 42–49), refused to see Christ as a merely individualistic savior. Christ, he showed, is the Last Adam who came to mend all that Adam broke. He is the only Son "who did, through His transcendent love, become what we are, that He might bring us to be even what He is Himself" (that is, to be sons of God).[5]

Athanasius later built on Irenaeus's work with an examination of what it means that our Savior is "the image of the invisible God" (Col. 1:15). Adam, he saw, was created "in the image of

---

4 Michael Reeves, foreword to Stephen Wellum, *Christ Alone: The Uniqueness of Jesus as Savior*, The Five Solas Series, ed. Matthew Barrett (Grand Rapids, MI: Zondervan, 2017), 13.

5 Irenaeus, *Against Heresies* 5.pref., in *The Apostolic Fathers with Justin Martyr and Irenaeus*, ed. Alexander Roberts, James Donaldson, and A. Cleveland Coxe, vol. 1 of *The Ante-Nicene Fathers* (Buffalo, NY: Christian Literature Company, 1885), 526.

God" and after his "likeness" (Gen. 1:26–27). It was, Athanasius explained, as if Adam was like a beautiful portrait painting: on him the image of God was drawn. And then, at the fall, it was as if this portrait was utterly wrecked. The image was ruined as Adam became vicious, selfish, and horribly unlike God. The question then became: How could this precious portrait be restored? There was nobody to restore it since there was nobody who knew what the portrait had once looked like. There was only one hope: The original subject of the portrait had to come and have his likeness redrawn on the canvas of humanity. Only the one whose likeness was originally drawn on Adam could restore and renew it. And so the Image of God himself came. He took humanity to renew his image in it.[6] Now in all this, Athanasius's entire presentation of this gospel story is dependent on the unique identity of Christ. In Christ alone can we be restored in the image of God. Only the Image of God himself can redeem us.

Then in the sixteenth century, the Reformers sought to reaffirm the biblical conviction that "there is one mediator between God and men, the man Christ Jesus" (1 Tim. 2:5), and that therefore "there is salvation in no one else, for there is no other name under heaven given among men by which we must be saved" (Acts 4:12). Their concern was that Peter had come to replace Christ as the rock and promised cornerstone on which the church is built. Grace was being portrayed as a blessing or benefit that could be abstracted from Christ, and faith described as a merit in itself. Thus, in the very earliest days of the Reformation, Luther wrote to his supervisor, Johann von Staupitz, "I teach that people should

---

6 For a fuller explanation, see Michael Reeves, "Only in Christ Can the Image of God Be Restored," Ligonier (website), July 15, 2020, https://www.ligonier.org/.

put their trust in nothing but Jesus Christ alone, not in their prayers, merits, or their own good deeds."[7]

To say that this principle has been vital for the church is not to say it has been easy to keep. Fallen sinners naturally gravitate toward anything but Jesus, even when that thing is religious. Christ can be eclipsed or added to by other gods or ideals, by works or by doctrines. C. S. Lewis's imagined demon Screwtape saw this with fiendish clarity when he wrote to his nephew:

My dear Wormwood,

The real trouble about the set your patient is living in is that it is *merely* Christian. They all have individual interests, of course, but the bond remains mere Christianity. What we want, if men become Christians at all, is to keep them in the state of mind I call "Christianity And". You know—Christianity and the Crisis, Christianity and the New Psychology, Christianity and the New Order, Christianity and Faith Healing, Christianity and Psychical Research, Christianity and Vegetarianism, Christianity and Spelling Reform. If they must be Christians let them at least be Christians with a difference. Substitute for the faith itself some Fashion with a Christian colouring.[8]

As Screwtape saw, to add to Christ is to cease to be *merely* Christian—to cease to be evangelical. It is an essential principle

---

7 Martin Luther, Letter to Johann von Staupitz (March 31, 1518), in *D. Martin Luthers Werke, Kritische Gesamtausgabe: Briefwechsel*, 18 vols. (Weimar: Hermann Böhlaus Nachfolger, 1930–1983), 1:160, quoted in Scott H. Hendrix, *Martin Luther: Visionary Reformer* (New Haven, CT: Yale University Press, 2017), 68.

8 C. S. Lewis, *The Screwtape Letters* (London: Geoffrey Bles, 1942), 126; emphasis original.

of evangelicalism, flowing from the very nature of the gospel, that (in the words of the Lausanne Covenant) "there is only one Savior and only one gospel."[9] J. C. Ryle saw that this principle can in fact be spoiled in two main ways:

> You may spoil the Gospel by *substitution*. You have only to withdraw from the eyes of the sinner the grand object which the Bible proposes to faith,—Jesus Christ; and to substitute another object in His place,—the Church, the Ministry, the Confessional, Baptism, or the Lord's Supper,—and the mischief is done. Substitute anything for Christ, and the Gospel is totally spoiled! Do this, either directly or indirectly, and your religion ceases to be Evangelical.
>
> You may spoil the Gospel by *addition*. You have only to add to Christ, the grand object of faith, some other objects as equally worthy of honour, and the mischief is done. Add anything to Christ, and the Gospel ceases to be a pure Gospel! Do this, either directly or indirectly, and your religion ceases to be Evangelical.[10]

Christ's identity is absolutely exclusive. For all our sinful strivings otherwise, nothing can in fact add to him or to his work. Therefore, we have no need "for any other prophet to provide us with a new authoritative revelation, any other priest to mediate between us and God, or any other king to rule his church."[11] As

---

9 The Lausanne Covenant, in John Stott, ed., *Making Christ Known: Historic Mission Documents from the Lausanne Movement 1974–1989* (Milton Keynes: Paternoster, 1997), 16.

10 Ryle, *Knots Untied*, 16.

11 Reeves, foreword to Wellum, *Christ Alone*, 13.

Scripture alone is our supreme authority, so Christ alone is our only hope. Only through him do we know the glory of the *living, triune* God.

The Sufficient Work of Christ

Just as the perfect nature of God ensures the perfection of his *word*, so the perfect nature of Christ ensures the perfection of his *work*. The gracious acts of God in both revelation and redemption are complete in Christ.

In revelation, he is the ultimate and unsurpassable word of God. So Hebrews begins,

> Long ago, at many times and in many ways, God spoke to our fathers by the prophets, but in these last days he has spoken to us by his Son, whom he appointed the heir of all things, through whom also he created the world. (Heb. 1:1–2)

That being the case, Jude can write of "the faith that was *once for all* [*hapax*] delivered to the saints" (Jude 3). And just the same word is used to describe his work of redemption. Christ was "offered *once* [*hapax*] to bear the sins of many" (Heb. 9:28). Peter writes that "Christ also suffered *once* [*hapax*] for sins" (1 Pet. 3:18).

In each verse, it is the adverb *hapax* that is used to describe the singularity and finality of what is found in Christ. *Hapax* or *ephapax* is a word used frequently in the New Testament of the work of Christ, especially in Hebrews as it contrasts the repeated (and so insufficient) sacrifices of the law with the single (and so sufficient) sacrifice of Christ. Here are some examples:

For the death he died he died to sin, *once for all* [*ephapax*], but the life he lives he lives to God. (Rom. 6:10)

He has no need, like those high priests, to offer sacrifices daily, first for his own sins and then for those of the people, since he did this *once for all* [*ephapax*] when he offered up himself. (Heb. 7:27)

He entered *once for all* [*ephapax*] into the holy places, not by means of the blood of goats and calves but by means of his own blood, thus securing an eternal redemption. (Heb. 9:12)

For since the law has but a shadow of the good things to come instead of the true form of these realities, it can never, by the same sacrifices that are continually offered every year, make perfect those who draw near. Otherwise, would they not have ceased to be offered, since the worshipers, having *once* [*hapax*] been cleansed, would no longer have any consciousness of sins? (Heb. 10:1–2)

And by that will we have been sanctified through the offering of the body of Jesus Christ *once for all* [*ephapax*]. (Heb 10:10)

After considering the biblical evidence, John Stott concluded,

It is because we have grasped the finality of what God has said and done in Christ that we evangelical people are determined to hold both fast. It is inconceivable to us that any truth could be revealed that is higher than what God has revealed in his own incarnate Son. It is equally inconceivable that anything should be deemed necessary to our salvation in addition to the cross.[12]

The word *ephapax* has a good claim to being the spark that ignited the Reformation in France. In October 1534, placards were posted in cities across France attacking the Roman Catholic Mass, using Hebrews 7:27: "He has no need, like those high priests, to offer sacrifices daily, first for his own sins and then for those of the people, since he did this *once for all* when he offered up himself." The point was that if Christ's sacrifice for sin on the cross was a complete work, "and thus neither need be nor can be repeated, then all our attempts to atone for sin must be both unnecessary and insulting to Christ, in that they suggest his work is not sufficient. If Christ's sacrifice was indeed 'once for all,' then there can be no need for other priests or high priests to offer up more." With that, the idea of an atoning Mass, and all our other attempts to atone for sin, were shown to be useless. "The only recourse was simple trust in Christ and his complete work."[13]

We are here right at the heart of what makes the good news good. Because Christ's redemptive work is entirely sufficient, the gospel is God's kind work of rescue, not his offer of assistance. It is not a call for the strong and good to prove themselves, but for the weak and bad to prove the depths of the mercy of Christ. Redemption is accomplished by Christ alone, and needs no topping up from us.

---

12 John Stott, *Evangelical Truth: A Personal Plea for Unity* (Leicester: IVP, 1999), 35.
13 Michael Reeves, *The Unquenchable Flame: Discovering the Heart of the Reformation* (Nashville, TN: B&H Academic, 2010), 98.

It is not only Christ's death: all of Christ's redemptive work is achieved without our contributing to it. It is one reason evangelicals have historically been so eager to defend the virgin birth, for it emphasizes the *miraculous* nature of our salvation. Mary did not produce the Savior of the world by herself. He was an unearned gift of God, given in the power of the Spirit. In other words, *we* have not joined God and man together. Salvation has not come from human effort or desire, but from heaven. Likewise with his resurrection and ascension and return: we do nothing; Christ does everything.

Yet it is Christ's death that is central to his redeeming work. It is the "hour" for which he came into the world (John 12:27). It is, above all, in his broken body and spilled blood that he wished to be remembered by his disciples. It is, therefore, classically evangelical to say with Paul, "Far be it from me to boast except in the cross of our Lord Jesus Christ" (Gal. 6:14). This is why evangelicals love to belt out the sort of words Charles Wesley penned to capture the meaning of Jesus's dying word, "It is finished" (John 19:30):

'Tis finished! The Messiah dies,
Cut off for sins, but not his own;
Completed is the sacrifice,
The great redeeming work is done.

'Tis finished! all the debt is paid;
Justice divine is satisfied,
The grand and full atonement made;
God for a guilty world has died.[14]

---

14 Charles Wesley, "'Tis Finished! The Messiah Dies," All The Lyrics (website), accessed September 9, 2021, https://www.allthelyrics.com/.

Wesley's words also express a classically evangelical under-standing of the cross. Evangelicals see that Scripture speaks of many facets of the cross: on the cross we see the glory and love of God displayed, and there Christ triumphs over the forces of evil. However, the cross is not *primarily* about stirring us with the love of God, or defeating Satan. From Genesis 3, the big question in Scripture has been: How can sinners, the children of Adam and Eve, be reconciled to God? The big problem has been the wrath of God at sin (Rom. 1:18). And from the Passover to the sacrifices of the law, the solution has always been a substitute, bearing the penalty of our sins in our place. Christ died *for* us, in our place, so that that "justice divine" might be satisfied and "we be saved by him from the wrath of God" (Rom. 5:8–9).

Martin Luther called this substitutionary work of atonement a "wonderful exchange," and explained as follows:

> This is that mystery which is rich in divine grace to sinners: wherein by a wonderful exchange our sins are no longer ours but Christ's: and the righteousness of Christ is not Christ's but ours. He has emptied himself of his righteousness that he might clothe us with it, and fill us with it: and he has taken our evils upon himself that he might deliver us from them.[15]

Yet such exchange language dates back to at least the second century, where the Letter to Diognetus uses it to emphasize the glorious sufficiency and completeness of Christ's work. There, the author writes that

---

15 Martin Luther, "Exposition of Psalm 21," in *D. Martin Luthers Werke, Kritische Gesamt-ausgabe: Briefwechsel*, 5:608.

when our wickedness had reached its height, and it had been clearly shown that its reward, punishment and death, was impending over us . . . [God] Himself took on Him the burden of our iniquities, He gave His own Son as a ransom for us, the holy One for transgressors, the blameless One for the wicked, the righteous One for the unrighteous, the incorruptible One for the corruptible, the immortal One for them that are mortal. For what other thing was capable of covering our sins than His righteousness? By what other one was it possible that we, the wicked and ungodly, could be justified, than by the only Son of God? O sweet exchange! O unsearchable operation! O benefits surpassing all expectation! that the wickedness of many should be hid in a single righteous One, and that the righteousness of One should justify many transgressors![16]

Justification by Faith Alone

If Christ's redeeming work really is entirely sufficient, then there is nothing for us to add. We have only to receive God's salvation with simple faith—and simple faith alone. Evangelicals have therefore seen justification by faith alone, which was *the* issue of the Reformation, as the litmus test of belief in the sufficiency of Christ as Redeemer. Indeed, declared Luther, "the church stands, if this article stands, and the church falls, if it falls."[17]

---

16 "The Epistle of Mathetes to Diognetus" 9.2–5, in *The Apostolic Fathers with Justin Martyr and Irenaeus*, ed. Alexander Roberts, James Donaldson, and A. Cleveland Coxe, vol. 1 of *The Ante-Nicene Fathers* (Buffalo, NY: Christian Literature Company, 1885), 28.

17 Martin Luther, *D. Martin Luthers Werke: Kritische Gesammtausgabe*, 120 vols. (Weimar, 1883–2009), 40.3:352. John Calvin similarly called justification by faith alone "the main hinge on which religion turns." John Calvin, *Institutes of the Christian Religion*,

The main passage on Luther's mind when he wrote those words was Romans 3:21–4:25, which he called "the chief point, and the very central place of the Epistle, and of the whole Bible."[18] Dr. Martyn Lloyd-Jones similarly described it as the "heart" of Paul's letter to the Romans because of how it gets to the nub of Paul's understanding of both atonement and justification.[19]

In the preceding chapters of Romans, Paul established that all humans are guilty and stand condemned under the wrath of God. But from Romans 3:21, he sets out the good news of how the righteousness of God is manifested:

> But now the righteousness of God has been manifested apart from the law, although the Law and the Prophets bear witness to it—the righteousness of God through faith in Jesus Christ for all who believe. For there is no distinction: for all have sinned and fall short of the glory of God, and are justified by his grace as a gift, through the redemption that is in Christ Jesus, whom God put forward as a propitiation by his blood, to be received by faith. This was to show God's righteousness, because in his divine forbearance he had passed over former sins. It was to show his righteousness at the present time, so that he might be just and the justifier of the one who has faith in Jesus. (Rom. 3:21–26)

---

ed. John T. McNeill, trans. Ford Lewis Battles, The Library of Christian Classics (Louisville, KY: Westminster John Knox, 1960), 3.11.1 (1:726).

18 Margin of the Luther Bible, on Rom. 3:23ff.

19 D. M. Lloyd-Jones, *Romans: An Exposition of Chapters 3:20–4:25, Atonement and Justification* (Edinburgh: Banner of Truth, 1970), xi.

Paul presents Christ as the full atoning sacrifice who dies for our sins so that God can be *both* the just Judge who does not overlook sin *and* the perfect Savior who gives his righteousness to those who have none. Because of that act of propitiation, God can declare sinners righteous "by his grace as a gift."

Paul can then go on to look at what justification means, and he takes Abraham—the father of the faithful—as his example:

> What then shall we say was gained by Abraham, our forefather according to the flesh? For if Abraham was justified by works, he has something to boast about, but not before God. For what does the Scripture say? "Abraham believed God, and it was counted to him as righteousness." Now to the one who works, his wages are not counted as a gift but as his due. And to the one who does not work but believes in him who justifies the ungodly, his faith is counted as righteousness. (Rom. 4:1–5)

In the gospel, God shows that he is a kind God who "justifies the *ungodly*." It was not that Abraham was considered righteous because he had actually been righteous himself: when he simply believed God in Genesis 15:6, he was *counted* as righteous. Abraham counted his own righteousness as nothing so that, as Paul said later, "I may gain Christ and be found in him, not having a righteousness of my own that comes from the law, but that which comes through faith in Christ, the righteousness from God that depends on faith" (Phil. 3:8–9).

To be justified, then, is to be a sinner on whom God has graciously pronounced the verdict "righteous." It is to be declared righteous, not with our own righteousness, but with Christ's. And Paul supports his point with David's words in Psalm 32:

> Blessed are those whose lawless deeds are forgiven,
>   and whose sins are covered;
> blessed is the man against whom the Lord will not count his
>   sin. (Rom. 4:7–8, quoting Ps. 32:1–2)

In other words, the blessed person is not a person who has no sin. The blessed person is the one whose sins are "covered," and against whom the Lord will not *count* his sin.

For evangelicals, all this is the familiar language of the Reformation. We expect to hear Luther and Calvin and other Reformers preaching justification by faith alone. But there is a common perception that before the Reformation there was very little clarity on the issue. It is as if we expect the early church fathers to stand—or thoughtlessly anticipate—the modern Roman Catholic Church in its view that "eternal life is, at one and the same time, grace and the reward given by God for good works and merits."[20] And if that is the case, then it is harder to stand by the claim that the evangelical faith is nothing but historic Christianity and true catholicity. If the church fathers did *not* teach justification by faith alone, the Reformers' claim to have attempted nothing but the renewal of ancient Christianity falls a little flat.

---

20 "Response of the Catholic Church to the Joint Declaration of the Catholic Church and the Lutheran World Federation on the Doctrine of Justification," Clarification 3, Pontifical Council for Promoting Christian Unity (website), accessed July 21, 2021, http://www.christianunity.va/content/unitacristiani/en.html.

However, it is simply not so. Here are just a few examples of the fathers speaking on justification, taken from what could be a very long list.[21] Tertullian (c. 155–230) was clear that God will "*impute* righteousness to those who believe in him, and make the just live through him, and *declare* the Gentiles to be his children *through faith*."[22] Basil of Caesarea (330–379) taught, "This is perfect and pure boasting in God, when one is not proud on account of his own righteousness but knows that he is indeed unworthy of the true righteousness and is justified *solely by faith in Christ*."[23] Another fourth-century theologian, Marius Victorinus, was equally emphatic when he affirmed: "We know that a man is not justified by the works of the law but through faith and the faith of Jesus Christ. . . . It is faith alone that gives justification and sanctification."[24] Or take the great preacher, John Chrysostom (c. 347–407), who proclaimed how God's grace "has allowed Him that did no wrong to be punished for those who had done wrong. . . . Him that was righteousness itself, 'He made sin,' that

21 See Nick Needham, "Justification in the Early Church Fathers," in *Justification in Perspective: Historical Developments and Contemporary Challenges*, ed. Bruce L. Mc-Cormack (Grand Rapids, MI: Baker Academic, 2006); Michael Horton, *Justification*, vol. 1 (Grand Rapids, MI: Zondervan, 2018), 39–91; James Buchanan, *The Doctrine of Justification* (Edinburgh, Banner of Truth, 1961), 31–113; Thomas C. Oden, *The Justification Reader* (Grand Rapids, MI: Eerdmans, 2002).

22 Tertullian, "The Five Books against Marcion" 5.3, in *Latin Christianity: Its Founder, Tertullian*, ed. Alexander Roberts, James Donaldson, and A. Cleveland Coxe, trans. Peter Holmes, vol. 3 of *The Ante-Nicene Fathers* (Buffalo, NY: Christian Literature Company, 1885), 435.

23 Quoted in Martin Chemnitz, *Examination of the Council of Trent*, vol. 1, trans. Fred Kramer (St. Louis, MO: Concordia, 2007), 505; emphasis added.

24 Marius Victorinus, Commentary on Galatians 2:15–16, in *Justification by Faith*, ed. H. George Anderson, T. Austin Murphy, and Joseph A. Burgess (Minneapolis, MN: Augsburg, 1985), 114.

is allowed Him to be condemned as a sinner, as one cursed to die" so that we might be not just "'righteous,' but 'righteousness,' indeed 'the righteousness of God.'"[25] In fact, while such clarity would become rarer from the fifth century on, in the early church it is those who confuse justification with sanctification who stand out as the eccentrics. Evangelicals thus stand in continuity with Scripture, the early church fathers, the Reformers, the Puritans, and eighteenth-century revivalists when they cherish justification by faith alone.

Justification by faith alone is at the centerground of the biblical gospel, the beautiful and essential consequence of the all-sufficiency of Christ the only Savior. As such, it is a doctrine that evangelicals love and tend with zeal. Yet if any of that gives the impression that evangelicals like to collect and pin up doctrines like dead butterflies, we need only look to evangelical hymnody. Through the centuries, evangelicals have not merely *admired* this doctrine, nor have they merely used it as a fence to mark out the true gospel. We *sing it out*, often, and often with tears in our eyes, for how it speaks of the majestic goodness of Christ and the sweet security we can have in him. Take just one example, "My Hope Is Built on Nothing Less" by Edward Mote (1836). Feel free to sing it out now!

My hope is built on nothing less
Than Jesus' blood and righteousness;
I dare not trust the sweetest frame,
But wholly lean on Jesus' name.

25 Chrysostom, Homilies on 2 Corinthians 11.5, as cited in Nick Needham, "Justification in the Early Church Fathers," 35.

On Christ, the solid Rock, I stand;
All other ground is sinking sand. . . .

When He shall come with trumpet sound,
Oh, may I then in Him be found,
Clothed in His righteousness alone,
Faultless to stand before the throne!
On Christ, the solid Rock, I stand;
All other ground is sinking sand.

4

Regeneration through the Spirit

"BUT WAIT," I hear the savvy reader cry, "haven't we been a bit too cerebral and propositional thus far? Isn't evangelicalism more than a list of doctrines?" Well, on the one hand, evangelicals are unapologetically people of truth and people of the book. Scripture is our guide and tells us of revealed truths from God. We can therefore sound quite "propositional" in how we insist on those truths. But that said, evangelicalism *is* more than a list of doctrines. It is more than bare orthodoxy. Dr. Martyn Lloyd-Jones, when defining what it is to be an evangelical, said, "We are not merely to define what is bare orthodoxy. You can have a dead orthodoxy. I am concerned to define the Evangelical in a way which goes beyond statements of belief."[1]

Lloyd-Jones was expressing a deep evangelical instinct we can understand if we return to Jesus's controversy with the Pharisees in Mark 7. In the middle of the scene, Jesus quotes Isaiah, saying,

---

1   D. M. Lloyd-Jones, *What Is an Evangelical?* (Edinburgh: Banner of Truth, 1992), 34.

"Well did Isaiah prophesy of you hypocrites, as it is written,

> "'This people honors me with their lips,
>> but their heart is far from me;
> in vain do they worship me,
>> teaching as doctrines the commandments of men.'"
>>> (Mark 7:6–7, quoting Isa. 29:13)

And just a few verses later, Jesus pushes into that theme of our hearts:

> And he called the people to him again and said to them, "Hear me, all of you, and understand: There is nothing outside a person that by going into him can defile him, but the things that come out of a person are what defile him. . . . For from within, out of the heart of man, come evil thoughts, sexual immorality, theft, murder, adultery, coveting, wickedness, deceit, sensuality, envy, slander, pride, foolishness. All these evil things come from within, and they defile a person." (Mark 7:14–15, 21–23)

Jesus knew how sin collapses religion into a hollow, outward show that fails to deal with the deep issues of the human heart. Thus, to be evangelical is to be highly wary of this pharisaical hypocrisy in which our lips may be orthodox, but our hearts are not. Evangelicals can never be about propositions *alone*: we want the theological truths of the gospel to *transform* us by the renewing of our minds (Rom. 12:2). It is why J. I. Packer could describe evangelicalism as "an ethos of convertedness within a larger ethos of catholicity."[2] It means we don't simply want to know truths about God. We want to know God, in a personal way. We don't simply *affirm* that Scripture is our supreme authority and that we are justified by faith alone through Christ alone. We actually *submit* to Scripture as our supreme authority and *enjoy* Christ as our only Savior, praising him from our hearts for his all-sufficiency and grace.

This essential feature of evangelicalism is commonly referred to as "conversionism," following David Bebbington.[3] Bebbington was quite right: the history of evangelicalism is indeed marked by story after story of conversion. However, *under* all those conversions lies the real evangelical principle: that of the need for the Spirit's *regeneration*.

I Once Was Lost

The first part of this principle is the confession of our dire *need*. It is a need expressed well by the first verse of John Newton's classic evangelical hymn, "Amazing Grace":

> Amazing grace! (how sweet the sound)
> That sav'd a wretch like me!
> I once was lost, but now am found,
> Was blind, but now I see.

Evangelicals love to sing those words as their own personal testimony, for we see ourselves as a saved people: once lost, once

---

2   J. I. Packer, "Reflections and Response," in *J. I. Packer and the Evangelical Future*, ed. T. George (Grand Rapids, MI: Baker, 2009), 182.

3   D. W. Bebbington, *Evangelicalism in Modern Britain: A History from the 1730s to the 1980s* (London: Unwin Hyman, 1989), 3.

blind. As J. C. Ryle made clear, a "leading feature in Evangelical Religion is *the depth and prominence it assigns to the doctrine of human sinfulness and corruption.*"[4]

What both Newton and Ryle have captured is that evangelicals do not simply think of themselves as once messy, once a touch wayward, or once a little spiritually slow on the uptake. We were, in the words of the apostle Paul,

> dead in the trespasses and sins in which you once walked,
> following the course of this world, following the prince of the
> power of the air, the spirit that is now at work in the sons of
> disobedience—among whom we all once lived in the passions
> of our flesh, carrying out the desires of the body and the mind,
> and were by nature children of wrath, like the rest of mankind.
> (Eph. 2:1–3)

Not just spiritually lame; we were spiritually dead. We were hostile to God (Rom. 8:7) because we instinctively loved the blinding darkness that covered our shame (John 3:19; 2 Cor. 4:4). It wasn't that we were all little Hitlers or Stalins, as utterly wicked as possible; we were quite capable of living lives of outward morality and respectability. But however good the outward appearance, inside we were hostile to God. We did not want him; we wanted sin.

Augustine spent much of the first half of his *Confessions* musing over what his lostness looked like, and his descriptions of his helpless floundering in sin never fail to resonate with evangelicals. For example:

---

4   J. C. Ryle, *Knots Untied* (London: Chas. J. Thynne, 1900), 4; emphasis original.

Look upon my heart, O God, look upon this heart of mine, on which you took pity in its abysmal depths. Enable my heart to tell you now what it was seeking in this action which made me bad for no reason, in which there was no motive for my malice except malice. The malice was loathsome, and I loved it. I was in love with my own ruin, in love with decay: not with the thing for which I was falling into decay but with decay itself, for I was depraved in soul, and I leapt down from your strong support into destruction, hungering not for some advantage to be gained by the foul deed, but for the foulness of it.[5]

In fact, the issue of our helpless addiction to sin was a driving cause of the Reformation. Luther himself called it "the essence of the matter in dispute . . . the question on which everything hinges . . . the vital spot."[6] Luther had been raised on the idea that we naturally have the ability to climb out of our sinfulness by ourselves. But his own painful experience and reading of Scripture had come to convince him otherwise. So it was that, in 1517, a few weeks before posting his famous Ninety-five Theses, he penned his foundational ninety-seven theses, in which he wrote,

Man is by nature unable to want God to be God. Indeed, he himself wants to be God, and does not want God to be God.

---

5 Augustine of Hippo, *The Confessions*, trans. Maria Boulding, ed. D. V. Meconi (San Francisco, CA: Ignatius, 1997), 2.4.9 (41).

6 Martin Luther, *Career of the Reformer III*, vol. 33 of *Luther's Works*, ed. Jaroslav Jan Pelikan, Hilton C. Oswald, and Helmut T. Lehmann (Philadelphia, PA: Fortress, 1999), 294.

. . . Therefore it is impossible to fulfil the law in any way without the grace of God.[7]

Being so unable in ourselves, Luther taught that we cannot make ourselves "righteous by doing righteous deeds"; we must be "*made righteous*" by God.[8] And for that, we need "the love of God, spread abroad in our hearts by the Holy Spirit."[9] Luther had come to see that we cannot save ourselves. Our problem lies too deep. Our hearts are simply inclined in the wrong direction, away from God, and all our effort will only ever follow that godless, self-deifying inclination. What we need is not more superficial self-improvement but a *radical* renewal: a new heart that will freely love and be pleased with God.

The New Birth

J. C. Ryle taught that another "leading feature in Evangelical Religion is the *high place which it assigns to the inward work of the Holy Spirit in the heart of man*."[10] It can hardly be seen as an eccentric feature, since the promise of a new heart given by the Spirit is a leading feature of the promise of the new covenant:

> "For this is the covenant that I will make with the house of Israel after those days, declares the LORD: I will put my law within them, and I will write it on their hearts. And I will be their God, and they shall be my people. And no longer shall each

7 Martin Luther, *Career of the Reformer I*, vol. 31 of *Luther's Works*, ed. Jaroslav Jan Pelikan, Hilton C. Oswald, and Helmut T. Lehmann (Philadelphia, PA: Fortress, 1999), 10–14.

8 Luther, *Career of the Reformer I*, 12.

9 Luther, *Career of the Reformer I*, 15.

10 Ryle, *Knots Untied*, 6; emphasis original.

one teach his neighbor and each his brother, saying, 'Know the Lord,' for they shall all know me, from the least of them to the greatest, declares the Lord. For I will forgive their iniquity, and I will remember their sin no more." (Jer. 31:33–34)

I will give you a new heart, and a new spirit I will put within you. And I will remove the heart of stone from your flesh and give you a heart of flesh. And I will put my Spirit within you, and cause you to walk in my statutes and be careful to obey my rules. (Ezek. 36:26–27)

Jesus could fairly tell Nicodemus, "Do not marvel that I said to you, 'You must be born again'" (John 3:7), for the necessity of new birth was the plain teaching and promise of the prophets. As the Spirit hovered over the waters in the beginning, giving life to creation, so we need the Spirit—the one the Nicene Creed calls "the giver of life"—to have new life. To be a Christian, we must be united to Christ, for then "if anyone is in Christ, he is a new creation. The old has passed away; behold, the new has come" (2 Cor. 5:17).

Do you not know that all of us who have been baptized into Christ Jesus were baptized into his death? We were buried therefore with him by baptism into death, in order that, just as Christ was raised from the dead by the glory of the Father, we too might walk in newness of life. (Rom. 6:3–4)

When a Christian is born again, they share in Christ's resurrection from the dead as the Father in his great mercy causes "us to be born again to a living hope through the resurrection of Jesus Christ from the dead" (1 Pet. 1:3).

This was something Augustine described eloquently in his *Confessions*. Having described his natural helplessness in sin, he then went on to describe his own experience of his heart being renewed by God:

> But you, Lord, are good and merciful, and your right hand plumbed the depths of my death, draining the cesspit of corruption in my heart, so that I ceased to will all that I had been wont to will, and now willed what you willed. But where had my power of free decision been throughout those long, weary years, and from what depth, what hidden profundity, was it called forth in a moment, enabling me to bow my neck to your benign yoke and my shoulders to your light burden, O Christ Jesus, my helper and redeemer? How sweet did it suddenly seem to me to shrug off those sweet frivolities, and how glad I now was to get rid of them—I who had been loath to let them go! For it was you who cast them out from me, you, our real and all-surpassing sweetness. You cast them out and entered yourself to take their place, you who are lovelier than any pleasure.[11]

It wasn't that Augustine had simply resolved to do better. Something in the very roots of his being had changed. God, by his Spirit, had turned his very desires so that he began to want and love God instead of sin, and hate sin instead of God.

Luther spoke similar language when he described his own "tower experience," reading Romans 1:17:

---

11 Augustine, *The Confessions*, 9.1.1 (226–27).

At last, by the mercy of God, meditating day and night, I gave heed to the context of the words, namely, "In it the righteousness of God is revealed, as it is written, 'He who through faith is righteous shall live.'" There I began to understand that the righteousness of God is that by which the righteous lives by a gift of God, namely by faith. And this is the meaning: the righteousness of God is revealed by the gospel, namely, the passive righteousness with which merciful God justifies us by faith, as it is written, "He who through faith is righteous shall live." *Here I felt that I was altogether born again and had entered paradise itself through open gates.*[12]

And it was apparently Luther's own work on Romans that "strangely warmed" John Wesley's heart. Wesley wrote in his journal for May 24, 1738:

In the evening I went very unwillingly to a society in Aldersgate-street, where one was reading Luther's preface to the Epistle to the Romans. About a quarter before nine, while he was describing the change which God works in the heart through faith in Christ, I felt my heart strangely warmed. I felt I did trust in Christ, Christ alone, for salvation; and an assurance was given me that He had taken away my sins, even mine, and saved me from the law of sin and death.[13]

---

12 Martin Luther, *Career of the Reformer IV*, vol. 34 of *Luther's Works*, ed. Jaroslav Jan Pelikan, Hilton C. Oswald, and Helmut T. Lehmann, (Philadelphia, PA: Fortress, 1999), 337; emphasis added.

13 John Wesley, *The Heart of Wesley's Journal: Illustrated*, intro. Robert E. Coleman (Grand Rapids, MI: Kregel, 1989), 43.

In a sermon on the new birth, Wesley later taught,

> If any doctrines within the whole compass of Christianity
> may be properly termed fundamental, they are doubtless these
> two,—the doctrine of justification, and that of the new birth:
> The former relating to that great work which God does *for us*,
> in forgiving our sins; the latter, to the great work which God
> does *in us*, in renewing our fallen nature.[14]

And very clearly, for both Luther and Wesley, it was the good
news of justification by faith alone that the Spirit used to give
them that new birth.

Evangelicals are people who are "born *of the Spirit*" (John 3:6,
8). To be an evangelical, then, means much more than to be born
into an evangelical culture or baptized in an evangelical church.
While water baptism is important to evangelicals as something
instituted and commanded by Jesus (Matt. 28:19), baptism does
not automatically cause this new birth. Baptism is a sign and seal
of the new birth, but we should never confuse the sign with the
thing signified. The new birth is a divine work of the Spirit, giving a new spiritual life and so effecting a radical change of heart.

To be clear, what is important is not the conversion *experience*
as such. Not all evangelicals feel they can point, like Luther and
Wesley, to the specific moment when God gave them new life.
What is important is the fact that God has given them new life,
and that new life shows itself in how they heartily repent of their
sin and heartily worship God. That, as it happens, is another

---

14 John Wesley, *Sermons on Several Occasions by John Wesley, M.A.*, 3 vols. (London: John
Mason, 1829), 2:65.

reason why it is more helpful to see "regeneration" rather than "conversionism" as the essential principle here. A focus on conversions could lead to a manipulative culture that works mainly to have more dramatic personal *experiences*. Evangelicalism at its best, however, has always seen the Spirit's regeneration as the vital matter. And true regeneration cannot be engineered by us: it is a divine work, brought about only through the gospel, which is "the power of God for salvation to everyone who believes" (Rom. 1:16).

The importance of regeneration also makes sense of another traditional evangelical concern: evangelism.[15] If people are naturally sinners who cannot save themselves but must be born again, then they need to hear the saving gospel. The people of the evangel see the vital need for the evangel to be shared and proclaimed. And evangelism is very much a fruit of the Spirit's regenerative work. On the very day of his resurrection, Jesus showed that evangelism is something that happens in the power of the Spirit.

> Jesus said to them again, "Peace be with you. As the Father has sent me, even so I am sending you." And when he had said this, he breathed on them and said to them, "Receive the Holy Spirit." (John 20:21–22)

The new life the Spirit gives is the life of the Son. The Spirit is, after all, the Spirit of the Son (Gal. 4:6). He therefore gives the children of God the heartbeat of the Son, so that they share his

---

15 J. I. Packer named evangelism as one of the six marks of evangelical faith in *The Evangelical Anglican Identity Problem: An Analysis* (Oxford: Latimer House, 1978), 20–23.

compassion and his concern for the world. Empowered by the Spirit, they speak the gospel out of the abundance of hearts that have been filled with the love of God (Matt. 12:34; Rom. 5:5).

The Manila Manifesto, produced by Lausanne II, the Second International Congress on World Evangelization in 1989, contains a paragraph entitled "God the Evangelist," which reads:

> The Scriptures declare that God himself is the chief evangelist. For the Spirit of God is the Spirit of truth, love, holiness and power, and evangelism is impossible without him. It is he who anoints the messenger, confirms the word, prepares the hearer, convicts the sinful, enlightens the blind, gives life to the dead, enables us to repent and believe, unites us to the body of Christ, assures us that we are God's children, leads us into Christ-like character and service, and sends us out in our turn to be Christ's witnesses. In all this the Holy Spirit's main preoccupation is to glorify Jesus Christ by showing him to us and forming him in us.[16]

The New Life

The Spirit does not give us a new birth as an end in itself: it is a new birth into a new and eternal life. He who began a good work in us will bring it to completion (Phil. 1:6), transforming us at every level into the image of Christ so that one day even our poor bodies will be like his glorious, resurrection body. And we, in turn, who live by the Spirit seek to keep in step with the Spirit (Gal. 5:25). And so, wrote J. C. Ryle, the "last leading feature

---

16 John Stott, ed., *Making Christ Known: Historic Mission Documents from the Lausanne Movement 1974–1989* (Milton Keynes: Paternoster, 1997), 238.

in Evangelical Religion is *the importance which it attaches to the outward and visible work of the Holy Ghost in the life of man.*"[17]

The apostle Paul describes this life in the Spirit in Romans 8:

There is therefore now no condemnation for those who are in Christ Jesus. For the law of the Spirit of life has set you free in Christ Jesus from the law of sin and death. For God has done what the law, weakened by the flesh, could not do. By sending his own Son in the likeness of sinful flesh and for sin, he condemned sin in the flesh, in order that the righteous requirement of the law might be fulfilled in us, who walk not according to the flesh but according to the Spirit. For those who live according to the flesh set their minds on the things of the flesh, but those who live according to the Spirit set their minds on the things of the Spirit. For to set the mind on the flesh is death, but to set the mind on the Spirit is life and peace. For the mind that is set on the flesh is hostile to God, for it does not submit to God's law; indeed, it cannot. (vv. 1–7)

It all starts with our freedom from condemnation in Christ. What we could not do by ourselves to fulfil the law, Christ has done, both fulfilling the commands of the law and receiving the condemnation our sin deserves (v. 3). But Christ did this, not that we might carry on as we were, but "in order that the righteous requirement of the law might be fulfilled *in us*" (v. 4).

And how is that requirement fulfilled *in us*? First, as we walk according to the Spirit (v. 4). We who have been set free from the

---

17 Ryle, *Knots Untied*, 7; emphasis original.

condemnation of the law actually begin to walk in accordance with the law, because of the Spirit's work in us. Our lives change. But more, something deeper happens, in our minds: "those who live according to the Spirit set their minds on the things of the Spirit" (v. 5). And it is worth unpacking this "something more" that the Spirit does in us. The first call of the law was "You shall love the LORD your God with all your heart and with all your soul and with all your might" (Deut. 6:5). Jesus called this "the great and first commandment. And a second is like it: You shall love your neighbor as yourself. On these two commandments depend all the Law and the Prophets." (Matt. 22:38–40). As Paul went on to explain, "Love is the fulfilling of the law" (Rom. 13:10). Without love for God and love for neighbor, the law would not be fulfilled in us, but this is the change the Spirit effects in believers.

There is therefore no such thing as a Christian who is *only* justified. Those to whom the Spirit gives new birth will live according to the Spirit and find themselves loving, thinking, and acting differently. For that reason, evangelicalism has never been about doctrine *alone*. Consistent evangelicals must *apply* their theology and so care about orthodoxy (right doctrine) *and* orthopraxy (right practice) *and* orthocardia (right heart). We are to be a people who do justice, love kindness, and walk humbly with our God (Mic. 6:8).

We have already heard from Augustine's *Confessions*, of his floundering in sin and his change of heart. He makes it very clear that the primary difference between his old life and his new was his love. As he explains it, we gravitate toward what we love, and from loving sin he had changed to loving God.

A body gravitates to its proper place by its own weight. This weight does not necessarily drag it downward, but pulls it to the place proper to it: thus fire tends upward, a stone downward. Drawn by their weight, things seek their rightful places. If oil is poured into water, it will rise to the surface, but if water is poured onto oil it will sink below the oil: drawn by their weight, things seek their rightful places. They are not at rest as long as they are disordered, but once brought to order they find their rest. Now, my weight is my love, and wherever I am carried, it is this weight that carries me.[18]

Ironically, while Martin Luther was an Augustinian friar, he initially failed to appreciate Augustine's insight, thinking that mere good works could fulfill the law. He therefore did practice his theology, but not in an evangelical way. What he eventually found, however, was that all his zealous effort only left him further from actually fulfilling the law by loving the Lord his God. Picturing God as grimly graceless, he admitted, "I did not love, yes, I hated the righteous God."[19] It was only when he understood the "no condemnation" of Romans 8:1 that he could understand what it really means to walk "according to the Spirit" (Rom. 8:4). Here's how he phrased it in his preface to Romans (yes, *that* preface that Wesley said he heard read out that night in Aldersgate Street):

How shall a work please God if it proceeds from a reluctant and resisting heart? To fulfil the law, however, is to do its works

18 Augustine, *The Confessions*, 13.9.10 (416).
19 Martin Luther, *Career of the Reformer IV*, 336.

with pleasure and love, to live a godly and good life of one's own accord, without the compulsion of the law. This pleasure and love for the law is put into the heart by the Holy Spirit.[20]

In other words, there is no true orthodoxy or orthopraxy without orthocardia. Evangelicals should therefore not be content with bare doctrine or bare religious behavior, however seemingly correct. Born of the Spirit, we should spurn both spiritual hypocrisy and emptiness, loving both God and neighbor as we "glory in Christ Jesus and put no confidence in the flesh" (Phil. 3:3).

The difference between an evangelical and a non-evangelical understanding of holiness can be seen well in a difference between the seventeenth-century Puritans and their contemporaries, the high-church Caroline Divines. Perhaps the most influential of the Carolines was William Laud (1573–1645), Charles I's Archbishop of Canterbury. Laud loved what he called "the beauty of holiness," by which he meant liturgical orderliness. He strictly insisted that the clergy must follow all the rubrics of the Church of England's prayer book, and was deeply concerned with clergy attire and the maintenance of church buildings and their physical beauty. And it was a particular sort of building he preferred: despising the Reformation—or "Deformation," as he called it—he preferred new churches to be built in the pre-Reformation, Gothic style, with an architectural emphasis on an altar instead of a communion table. For, he said, "the altar is the greatest place of God's residence upon earth, greater than the pulpit; for there 'tis *Hoc est corpus meum*, This is my body; but in the other it is at most but *Hoc est verbum*

---

20   Martin Luther, *Word and Sacrament I*, vol. 35 of *Luther's Works*, ed. Jaroslav Jan Pelikan, Hilton C. Oswald, and Helmut T. Lehmann (Philadelphia, PA: Fortress, 1999), 368.

meum, This is my word."[21] It was all most revealing of his theology. His preference for altars over pulpits always tended toward an emphasis on the necessity of ongoing priestly mediation by the clergy as opposed to an emphasis on the completed work of Christ. But also, that emphasis on ceremony, architecture, and correct liturgical procedure reflected the Caroline idea that we change *from the outside in.* The stress, then, would not be placed on the need for personal faith but on the need for external things to be done rightly. Right dress, right act, and right behavior were the prime concern.

In contrast, while the Puritans valued liturgy (it was, after all, a Reformer who had written their first prayer book), and while they never wanted their actions to be misconstrued, they were less concerned with ritual because they saw that the gospel works in another way. Our first need, they would emphasize, is not correct behavior but a new birth and a new heart that loves God. Conversion of the heart, they held, was more vital than maintenance of a particular practice, for the Spirit changes us not from the outside-in, but *from the inside-out.* As a result, the Puritans prioritized preaching that would win hearts away from sin and to Christ. For them, therefore, pulpits took priority: pulpits where the gospel that is the power of God to turn hearts could be proclaimed. One of their number, Richard Sibbes, explained,

The outward is easy, and subject to hypocrisy. It is an easy matter to rend clothes and to force tears, but it is a hard matter to

---

21 Nicholas Tyacke, "Puritanism, Arminianism and Counter-revolution," in *Reformation to Revolution: Politics and Religion in Early Modern England,* ed. Margo Todd (London and New York: Routledge, 1995), 64.

afflict the soul. The heart of man taketh the easiest ways, and lets the hardest alone, thinking to please God with that. But God will not be served so; for he must have the inward affections, or else he doth abhor the outward actions. Therefore let us as well labour for humble hearts as humble gestures. We must rend our hearts and not our clothes, when we come into the presence of God.[22]

Outward and visible holiness they wanted, but only if rooted in the heart, not if it was a superficial show.

The New People

In practice, sadly, evangelicals have often tended to be individualists in their faith. But again, our understanding of what it is to be truly evangelical should not be taken from evangelical practice but the evangel. Evangelicals are people who have been born again, but to be born again is to be born or baptized *into* Christ (Rom. 6:3; Gal. 3:27). From the moment of our regeneration, we are part of a bigger whole, the body of Christ (Rom 12:5; 1 Cor. 12:13).

It means that, as J. I. Packer noted, an important part of our new life in the Spirit is our fellowship in the body of Christ.[23] But for that fellowship to be truly *evangelical*, it must be the evangel that brings the unity, and not any other agenda or identity. So the apostle Paul wrote to the Gentiles in Ephesus of how Jews and Gentiles are brought together in Christ:

22 Richard Sibbes, *The Complete Works of Richard Sibbes*, ed. A. B. Grosart, 7 vols. (Edinburgh: James Nichol, 1862), 6:61.

23 Packer, *The Evangelical Anglican Identity Problem*, 20–23.

For he himself is our peace, who has made us both one and has broken down in his flesh the dividing wall of hostility by abolishing the law of commandments expressed in ordinances, that he might create in himself one new man in place of the two, so making peace, and might reconcile us both to God in one body through the cross, thereby killing the hostility. And he came and preached peace to you who were far off and peace to those who were near. For through him we both have access in one Spirit to the Father. So then you are no longer strangers and aliens, but you are fellow citizens with the saints and members of the household of God, built on the foundation of the apostles and prophets, Christ Jesus himself being the cornerstone. (Eph. 2:14–20)

Christ Jesus is the cornerstone of the fellowship, and his teaching the foundation of its unity. And so it must be for those who have no boast except the cross of our Lord Jesus Christ (Gal. 6:14): there can be no second class and no segregation in Christ's church.

This is not easy or natural for us, since we all come into the church with our own particular cultural identity, an identity we easily confuse with the gospel. And so the church can appear to be just another club defined by ethnicity or class or politics. But, as Conrad Mbewe writes, "we must never limit our church's membership to one tribe or one ethnic group."[24] To the extent that our church is defined by such identities, it is not *evangelical*. Therefore, just as evangelicals will fight their own individual sin as they keep in step with the Spirit, so we must fight the collective

24 Conrad Mbewe, *God's Design for the Church: A Guide for African Pastors and Ministry Leaders* (Wheaton, IL: Crossway, 2020), 31.

sin of allowing anything but the gospel to be the cause of our unity. We must live out the truth that all who are born again are one in Christ Jesus, and one *only* in Christ Jesus, not by any other identity (Gal. 3:27–28). Only then do we testify that the gospel is the hope for world peace, bringing Jew and Gentile, male and female, black and white, rich and poor, all together into the loving household of God.

The Importance of Being Gospel People

THE NEW TESTAMENT has a good deal to say about the importance of being gospel people.

Paul's letter to the Romans, for example, is a New Testament book all about the *gospel* and about being *gospel people*. In the first eleven chapters, Paul lays out the "gospel of God, which he promised beforehand through his prophets in the holy Scriptures" (1:1–2). It is good news "concerning his Son" (1:3), the Last Adam (5:12–21), our only hope. And it is good news concerning "the redemption that is in Christ Jesus, whom God put forward as a propitiation by his blood" (3:24–25). In Romans, we read that

"none is righteous, no, not one;
no one understands;
no one seeks for God.
All have turned aside; together they have become worthless."
(3:10–12)

Yet, those lost in sin (8:7) can "be saved by him from the wrath of God" (5:9). Sinners can be "justified by his grace as a gift, through the redemption that is in Christ Jesus" (3:24). Through the gospel, they can be born again, united to Christ in his death and resurrection (6:3–4) to enjoy no condemnation (8:1) and a new life, walking "according to the Spirit" (8:4). Such people—whether Jew or Gentile—who heartily believe in Jesus become the true people of God, the people who have attained the "righteousness that is by faith" (9:30; cf. 10:9–13).

At the risk of oversimplifying, we could summarize the first eleven chapters of Romans like this:

- Chapters 1–4 concern the Son's once-and-for-all redemption of lost sinners so that they might be justified by grace alone.
- Chapters 5–8 concern the Spirit's work of regeneration, how he gives new birth to the dead and new life to sinners who will then walk in the Spirit.
- Chapters 9–11 concern the Father's word of revelation, being a scriptural defense of the statement that "it is not as though the word of God has failed" (Rom. 9:6).

Then, from chapter 12, Paul appeals to the Roman Christians to live as transformed, gospel people. Especially, he calls them, *amid their differences* (12:3–8), to "love one another with brotherly affection" (12:10; also 12:13–21; 13:8–14). Paul recognizes that while they share a common gospel, they will differ over a number of other matters (e.g., what to eat and special days), and he asks them not to judge or grieve each other over such matters (chap. 14). What is striking is the complete difference of tone from that in Galatians 1, where Paul sees the Galatians turning to "a different gospel" (Gal. 1:6). For Paul, to change the gospel is intolerable: "even if we or an angel from heaven should preach to you a gospel contrary to the one we preached to you, let him be accursed" (1:8). But in Romans 14, it is not the gospel that is the cause of disagreement. The gospel is not a matter over which we can cheerfully diverge. Yet the people of the gospel, while never turning from the gospel itself, should clearly exercise some latitude over many other issues over which Christians differ. In fact, they should actively "watch out for those who cause divisions and create obstacles" (16:17). That is what it means to be people of the *gospel* rather than people of a party.

Similar notes can be heard in 1 Corinthians. There, Paul addresses the death and resurrection of Christ as matters "of first importance" (15:3). Yet the first—and seemingly most basic—exhortation of the letter is this: "I appeal to you, brothers, by the name of our Lord Jesus Christ, that all of you agree, and that there be no divisions among you, but that you be united in the same mind and the same judgment" (1:10). To a highly tribal church riven by the cries of "I follow Paul" or "I follow Apollos" or "I follow Cephas" or "I follow Christ" (1:12), Paul calls for unity in Christ alone and the word of the cross (1:13–31). While the gospel must never be compromised by our actions (chaps. 5–6) or our beliefs (chap. 15), Paul calls for a unity found in the gospel (11:17–14:40) that does not depend on complete agreement on all things (chap. 8). In that way, we prove that we are not of a sect but of the gospel.

The Gospel, Our Anchor

For people of the gospel, the gospel serves as our mooring anchor. An anchor stops a ship from drifting while allowing it a certain amount of movement on the surface of the water. Just so, the gospel holds us to Scripture's matters of first importance while allowing some slack for differences of opinion on other matters. As Paul called the Romans and Corinthians to unity in the gospel and liberty in what to eat, so the anchor keeps us from making shipwreck of our faith (1 Tim 1:19) without making our every disagreement a cause for schism.

With the gospel as our anchor, evangelicals are able to see that not every issue is a gospel issue, and not every error (or departure from our view or practice) is a soul-killing heresy. Some doctrines are more essential and foundational than others (Heb. 5:12–14). Henry Venn argued that recognition of this was in fact a distinguishing mark of evangelical thought. Evangelicals, he wrote, are marked out "not so much in their systematic statement of doctrines, as in the relative importance which they assign to the particular parts of the Christian System, and in the vital operation of the Christian Doctrines upon the heart and conduct."[1] This, added J. C. Ryle, is the only true way to be gospel people:

You may spoil the Gospel by *disproportion*. You have only to attach an exaggerated importance to the secondary things of Christianity, and a diminished importance to the first things, and the mischief is done. Once alter the proportion of the parts of truth, and truth soon becomes downright error! Do this, either directly or indirectly, and your religion ceases to be Evangelical.[2]

1   Henry Venn, ed., *The Life and a Selection from the Letters of the late Rev. Henry Venn, M.A.* (London, 1835), vii–viii. See also J. C. Ryle, *Knots Untied* (London: Chas. J. Thynne, 1900), 8.
2   J. C. Ryle, *Knots Untied*, 17; emphasis original.

To be evangelical thus means to be called to exercise biblical wisdom. As J. I. Packer put it, it involves the need to discern between "the virtue of tolerating different views on secondary issues on the basis of clear agreement on essentials" and "the vice of retreating from the light of Scripture into an intellectual murk where no outlines are clear, all cats are grey, and syncretism is the prescribed task."[3]

Walking with such discernment is no easy task, and describing how to do so well takes more than a few pages.[4] Yet Albert Mohler uses a helpful metaphor for evangelical thinking here: that of theological triage.[5] Triage is a sorting system commonly used in medical contexts to decide in an emergency which injuries must be treated first. It ensures that a gunshot wound is treated with more urgency than a scraped knee. *Theological* triage recognizes that some doctrines are first-level issues, essential to the gospel. These are the sorts of doctrines we have looked at in this book: the nature and identity of the triune God, the Father's revelation, the Son's redemption, and the Spirit's regeneration. Other doctrines are not necessarily unimportant because they are nonessential. Some are second-level issues, like baptism and church government, which, while not essential to the gospel, still cause Christians to separate into various denominations. Some

---

3 J. I. Packer, "Taking Stock in Theology," in *Evangelicals Today*, ed. John C. King (Lutterworth, 1973), 17.

4 For readers interested in pursuing this further, I recommend two books: Gavin Ortlund, *Finding the Right Hills to Die On: The Case for Theological Triage* (Wheaton, IL: Crossway, 2020); and Rhyne R. Putnam, *When Doctrine Divides the People of God: An Evangelical Approach to Theological Diversity* (Wheaton, IL: Crossway, 2020).

5 For instance, see R. Albert Mohler Jr., *The Disappearance of God: Dangerous Beliefs in the New Spiritual Openness* (Colorado Springs, CO: Multnomah, 2009), 1–8.

are third-level doctrines like different views on the timing of the return of Christ: they are significant, but issues over which Christians may disagree and still remain in close fellowship, even within the same local congregation.[6] Second- and third-level doctrines *still matter*, but they must not be given an exaggerated importance. And then there are some other (fourth-level) issues that are actually relatively unimportant, such as what we eat.

Since being gospel people means both unwavering faithfulness to the gospel *and* a refusal to elevate other issues to the level of the gospel, evangelicals have to walk a line between fighting over too much and discerning too little. Time and again, we have failed—and been shot at from both sides for our failures. But our failures do not invalidate the goodness of the task. Loyalty to the gospel demands that we work simultaneously against both tribalism and the muddying of theological waters.

Splintering and Blurring

Worldwide, we evangelicals have much to repent of here. We have been guilty of a balkanizing tendency to segregate into like-minded ghettos, having fellowship only with those who agree with us on second- and even third-level issues. Or political preferences. Or cultural assumptions. *And* we have been guilty of compromising the gospel by erasing its distinctives to achieve some form of sub-evangelical "gospel-lite" unity.

We all probably tend to either one error or the other. Conservatives tend to fear theological blurring most. A clear example of such unacceptable downgrading of the gospel would be the 1999

---

6   Albert Mohler, "A Call for Theological Triage and Christian Maturity," Albert Mohler (website), July 12, 2005, https://albertmohler.com/.

Joint Declaration on the Doctrine of Justification, signed by the Roman Catholic Church and the Lutheran World Federation. In the Joint Declaration, both parties claimed that they were "now able to articulate a common understanding of our justification by God's grace through faith in Christ."[7] This was an impressive claim, and one that purported to sidestep the old doctrinal condemnations of the Council of Trent (1545–1563), which said,

> CANON IX.-If any one saith, that by faith alone the impious is justified; in such wise as to mean, that nothing else is required to co-operate in order to the obtaining the grace of Justification, and that it is not in any way necessary, that he be prepared and disposed by the movement of his own will; let him be anathema. CANON XI.-If any one saith, that men are justified, either by the sole imputation of the justice of Christ, or by the sole remission of sins, to the exclusion of the grace and the charity which is poured forth in their hearts by the Holy Ghost, and is inherent in them; or even that the grace, whereby we are justified, is only the favour of God; let him be anathema. CANON XII.-If any one saith, that justifying faith is nothing else but confidence in the divine mercy which remits sins for Christ's sake; or, that this confidence alone is that whereby we are justified; let him be anathema. CANON XXIV.-If any one saith, that the justice received is not preserved and also increased before God through good works; but that the said works are merely the fruits and signs

---

7 "Joint Declaration on the Doctrine of Justification," par. 5, Pontifical Council for Promoting Christian Unity (website), accessed July 21, 2021, http://www.christian unity.va/content/unitacristiani/en.html.

of Justification obtained, but not a cause of the increase thereof; let him be anathema.[8]

Yet in light of those condemnations, the Joint Declaration's understanding of justification was not that sinners are saved by faith alone without works by the sole remission of sins and the sole imputation of the righteousness of Christ. It therefore could not amount to the evangelical understanding of justification that the Council of Trent sought so carefully to define and oppose.[9] Furthermore, the official *Catechism of the Catholic Church* still teaches that "justification is not only the remission of sins, but also the sanctification and renewal of the inner man. Justification *detaches man from sin* which contradicts the love of God, and purifies his heart of sin."[10] Now if it were true that justification is a process that included our sanctification and inner renewal, the Catechism would be quite right to conclude that we can therefore qualify ourselves for eternal life. But such an understanding simply cannot be squared with an evangelical understanding of justification whereby I am given the righteous status of Christ without that status being in any way dependent upon the state of my heart or life. "Where evangelicalism views justification as a divine declarative act whereby God pronounces the sinner righteous in Christ, Rome still sees justification as an ongoing,

---

8   *The Canons and Decrees of the Sacred and Oecumenical Council of Trent*, trans. J. Waterworth (London: Dolman, 1848), 45–47.

9   See Michael Reeves in "The Joint Declaration on the Doctrine of Justification: A Curtain on the Reformation?," Union (website), accessed September 9, 2021, https://www.uniontheology.org/.

10   Catholic Church, *Catechism of the Catholic Church*, pars. 1989–90, Vatican (website), accessed July 21, 2021, https://www.vatican.va/content/vatican/en.html.

transformative, and cooperative process."[11] That being the case, it is deluded or deceitful to imagine that the Joint Declaration has proven anything like an end to the important theological differences between evangelicals and the Roman Catholic Church. The matter of the Reformation still stands: are believers justified through faith in Christ *alone*, as evangelicals maintain, or is eternal life, as Rome teaches, "at one and the same time, grace and the reward given by God for good works and merits"?[12]

However, while theological conservatives are less likely to countenance such downgrade, they are more likely to fall into the other ugly and opposing evangelical error: the *rabies theologorum*. When Luther's friend Philip Melanchthon (1497–1560) lay dying, he wrote of his happiness that he would soon be free of the *rabies theologorum* or "madness of the theologians." By this he meant the tendency of theologians to be always snapping at each other like rabid dogs. It is the prickly inclination to allow second- and third-level issues to trump the rallying cry of the gospel.

And it is hardly as if theologians alone are guilty here. For it is not theology alone that divides evangelicals. Far, far from it. Personalities, culture, and politics can equally trump the gospel. Evangelical tribalism is all too often not about doctrinal disagreement at all (however much it masquerades as such). Evangelical people, churches, and ministries can *use* theology to cloak the actual personal or political reasons why they do not have the

---

11 Reeves in "The Joint Declaration on the Doctrine of Justification: A Curtain on the Reformation?"

12 "Response of the Catholic Church to the Joint Declaration of the Catholic Church and the Lutheran World Federation on the Doctrine of Justification," Clarification 3, Pontifical Council for Promoting Christian Unity (website), accessed July 21, 2021, http://www.christianunity.va/content/unitacristiani/en.html.

degree of fellowship that their shared belief encourages. True evangelicalism should mean we can enjoy hearty fellowship with other evangelicals without ever imagining that our fellowship implies our approval of everything they believe. But when loyalty to the gospel wanes, culture- or personality-shaped empires mushroom where members of each tribe fear any association with outsiders because their association might be read as an endorsement of all the outsider's alternative views. In such situations, precisely because the gospel is not the unifying factor, people become increasingly blind to the distinction between gospel issues and cultural differences. I never forget the story that Norwegian friends told me of some theological conference in Norway. Into the conference walked a woman wearing makeup. The men were so shocked they dropped their cigars into their beers. It hadn't crossed their minds that their own smoking and drinking might be surprising or offensive to other Christians; what unsettled them was the makeup that in other Christian contexts would be considered quite normal. Culture, rather than the gospel, had become normative.

Carl Henry went so far as to lament that

> evangelicals often seem to be one of the most divided and divisive forces in the ecclesiastical world even in their internal dealings. Splits, suspicions, wordy campaigns are common features. Squabbling about less essential matters seems to absorb the energy that should go to working together on essentials.[13]

---

13 Carl F. H. Henry, "A Plea for Evangelical Unity (1961)," in *Architect of Evangelicalism: The Essential Essays of Carl F. H. Henry*, The Best of Christianity Today (Bellingham, WA: Lexham, 2019), 30.

In sharp and beautiful contrast, Charles Spurgeon exemplified the evangelical spirit in how he would speak of John Wesley. As a Calvinist, Spurgeon abhorred Wesley's Arminianism; and yet he refused to write Wesley off. He saw him as a flawed evangelical hero from whom all evangelicals can learn. It meant that he refused to indulge in any sectarian cult of Wesley, which he knew would anger some: "unless you can give him constant adulation, unless you are prepared to affirm that he had no faults, and that he had every virtue, even impossible virtues, you cannot possibly satisfy his admirers."[14] But Spurgeon was sterner still in his refusal to indulge a Calvinist sectarian vilification of Wesley:

> To ultra-Calvinists his name is as abhorrent as the name of the Pope to a Protestant: you have only to speak of Wesley, and every imaginable evil is conjured up before their eyes, and no doom is thought to be sufficiently horrible for such an archheretic as he was. I verily believe that there are some who would be glad to rake up his bones from the tomb and burn them, as they did the bones of Wycliffe of old—men who go so high in doctrine, and withal add so much bitterness and uncharitableness to it, that they cannot imagine that a man can fear God at all unless he believes precisely as they do.[15]

Both Calvinists and Arminians should be able to appreciate the gospel-anchored wisdom and sensitivity Spurgeon shows here. It teaches us that we can uphold the gospel with faithfulness and

---

14 C. H. Spurgeon, *The Two Wesleys* (London: Passmore and Alabaster, 1861), 4.
15 Spurgeon, *The Two Wesleys*, 4.

oppose error while at the same time heeding J. C. Ryle's warning that "we do not condemn men too strongly for not seeing all things in our point of view, or excommunicate and anathematize them because they do not pronounce our shibboleth."[16] For a true evangelical spirit has both a strong doctrinal backbone and a body of wisdom and grace.

A Rope of Sand?

Some wonder whether the difficult path of evangelical discernment is one worth travelling. Certainly, it would be easier for us all to abandon the attempt and retreat into silos where everyone agrees with us on almost everything. That would be a comfortable position to take, allowing everyone to settle into their own particular culture. But such blithe lack of concern for Christian unity is not health as measured by the gospel. Jesus's own desire, the night before his crucifixion, was that believers "may all be one, just as you, Father, are in me, and I in you, that they also may be in us, so that the world may believe that you have sent me" (John 17:21). Carl Henry commented on Jesus's prayer,

> No matter how loudly we proclaim our attachment to Scripture, we do it poor service, and gain ourselves little credence, if in our actions we flagrantly disregard the will of God therein revealed. Once the declared will of Jesus Christ is known, no other motive is needed. It is the delight and privilege of the sheep to hear and obey the Shepherd's voice.[17]

16 J. C. Ryle, *Christian Leaders of the Last Century; or England a Hundred Years Ago* (London: T. Nelson, 1869), 85.

17 Henry, "A Plea for Evangelical Unity," 31.

Christ then shed his blood—the heart of our gospel—to reconcile us together to God:

> But now in Christ Jesus you who once were far off have been brought near by the blood of Christ. For he himself is our peace, who has made us both one and has broken down in his flesh the dividing wall of hostility by abolishing the law of commandments expressed in ordinances, that he might create in himself one new man in place of the two, so making peace, and might reconcile us both to God in one body through the cross, thereby killing the hostility. (Eph. 2:13–16)

That is why Paul can devote his letter to the Romans to expounding the gospel that unites while calling them to "love one another with brotherly affection" (12:10) amid their other differences and "watch out for those who cause divisions and create obstacles" (16:17). According to the gospel, unity—not sectarianism—is health.

Part of the difficulty with evangelical unity is that we instinctively tend to picture unity institutionally. This is how it is in Roman Catholicism, where unity is *structural* or *organizational*: to be united to Christ means to be a member of the Roman Catholic Church. This holds an understandable appeal to evangelicals disillusioned by their doctrinal disarray: the historic structures and long traditions of the Roman Catholic and Orthodox churches seem to hold out the possibility of the tangible, historic, and worldwide unity they long for. Such structural unity can *look* more robust to withstand error. Compared to that, evangelicalism can *look* fractious and fragile.

Evangelicals, however, believe that real unity must run deeper. Organizational unity does not make the kind of unity for which Christ prayed. After all, someone may be a member of a local church without being born again or savingly united to Christ. For now, the wheat and the tares are mixed together. When evangelicals hear Jesus praying that we may all be one, we do not imagine him dreaming of a monolithic institution but a *spiritual* unity. That unity will manifest itself in practical expressions of fellowship and partnership, but, as Iain Murray put it, "Spiritual unity does not demand oneness in organization." Indeed, he goes on, "to put an external unity before essential truths (without which there is no church at all) is inconsistent with being an evangelical."[18] And in any case, is it really true that institutional unity is more robust against error or division? The Roman Catholic Church has maintained an impressive institutional unity through space and time while denying, for example, the supremacy of Scripture and the complete sufficiency of Christ's once-and-for-all sacrifice on the cross. And are such institutions really more unanimous? D. A. Carson writes,

> I am frankly astonished that anyone could think that evangelical theology is more diverse than denominational theology or the theology of a certain broadly based heritage. Published Presbyterian theology today varies from Westminster confessionalism to flat-out anti-supernaturalism, with every conceivable stopping-place in between. And off on one side, ordained Presbyterian ministers insist that Sophia is a feminine expression of God,

18 Iain Murray, *Evangelicalism Divided: A Record of Crucial Change in the Years 1950 to 2000* (Edinburgh: Banner of Truth, 2000), 289.

adopt pantheistic views, and espouse reincarnation. What is called Reformed thought is just as varied; the holiness and charismatic traditions scarcely less so. In any case, it is always unfair to compare the best of one tradition with the worst of another.[19]

Five hundred years ago, the Roman Catholic Church warned the Reformers that their rejection of the authority of the pope would mean their movement would quickly shatter into a thousand factions. But now, the evidence of those centuries past has disproved the charge. Half a millennium on, evangelicalism is not hopelessly fragmented. The evidence can be seen in J. I. Packer and Thomas Oden's book, *One Faith: The Evangelical Consensus*.[20] Surveying some seventy-five evangelical documents, including the Lausanne Covenant (1974), the Manila Manifesto (1989), and The Amsterdam Declaration (2000), they demonstrate that among those who *maintain* the label evangelical there is an impressive theological consensus. The authority of the Bible—and sometimes it has been, quite literally, the Bible alone they have had—has directed millions of believers to share the same gospel essentials taught by Paul, Luther, and Newton.

That theological consensus has been the foundation needed for centuries of cross-denominational evangelistic effort. Evangelical unity in the gospel has been life-giving and fruitful. Baptist pastors in Poland, Anglican ministers in Australia, Presbyterian ministers in Scotland, and Independent pastors in China who have never

---

19 D. A. Carson, *The Gagging of God: Christianity Confronts Pluralism* (Leicester: Apollos, 1996), 455.

20 J. I. Packer and Thomas Oden, *One Faith: The Evangelical Consensus* (Downers Grove, IL: InterVarsity Press, 2004).

met and have no organizational link happily send funds to each other's missionary efforts, confident that they are serving and heralding the same essential gospel.[21] And where would all the evangelical parachurch mission organizations be without that confidence? Indeed, argue Kenneth Collins and Jerry Walls,

> Evangelical Protestantism, with all its denominational diversity, actually represents a far more impressive model of true unity than does the Church of Rome. The National Association of Evangelicals is composed of some forty different evangelical churches. Despite their differences on secondary issues, there is genuine agreement and substantial unity on classic ortho- dox catholic doctrine. Most of these churches, moreover, are in communion with each other. In the same vein, it is a safe bet that there is far more genuine agreement about catholic Christianity among the members of the Evangelical Theologi- cal Society than there is among, say, members of the Catholic Theological Society of America.[22]

21 Such international, cross-denominational partnership in the gospel is quintessentially evangelical. Conrad Mbewe writes, "We must not think of the church primarily in terms of our own local church or denomination. We belong to the body of Christ that encompasses the whole planet. The church is in Africa, in America, in Europe, in Asia, and so on. It is everywhere. Your local church is only a local manifestation of this big, international body. There is sometimes such an emphasis on being an 'African church' that we can easily lose sight of the fact that we are one body—one church—right across the globe. Our local church should be in partnership with other churches in fulfilling the task that Jesus has given to his worldwide church. Our local church should also be actively helping weaker churches around us to become stronger." Conrad Mbewe, *God's Design for the Church: A Guide for African Pastors and Ministry Leaders* (Wheaton, IL: Crossway, 2020), 30–31.

22 Kenneth J. Collins and Jerry L. Walls, *Roman but Not Catholic: What Remains at Stake 500 Years after the Reformation* (Grand Rapids, MI: Baker, 2017), 399.

Evangelicals and Denominations

If evangelicals seek a manifested spiritual unity, what should they make of all our denominations? They cannot believe that the unity Jesus desires comes from the organizational uniting of denominations, for true unity is not merely structural. They will surely seek to purify the church by the word of God, but they will not dream of a single, united evangelical church or denomination. Evangelicalism is by definition cross-denominational. For, to have the wisdom of Paul in Romans means recognizing the difference between first- and second-level issues, and that local churches, denominations, and organizations need agreement on various second-level matters (such as church government) that the gospel itself does not demand. Iain Murray explains,

> Evangelicalism stands for the saving essentials of Christian belief. But it has never claimed that such a minimum of belief is all that is necessary for the full life and organization of churches. The whole counsel of God contains more than that minimum and how that counsel is to be understood at certain points has been the subject of prolonged disagreement among those who are united in accepting the rule of Scripture.[23]

It is not that evangelicals *do not care* about theological matters beyond the saving essentials of Christian belief. Nor does it mean we neglect such issues to adopt a vapid one-size-fits-all identity. It is a false antithesis to be forced to choose between Presbyterianism or Episcopalianism or Independency and evangelicalism.

---

23 Murray, *Evangelicalism Divided*, 278.

Evangelicals can and should be good and eager confessional members of their local church or denomination, with all its particular doctrinal requirements.

Yet to be people of the gospel means putting insistence on the gospel before insistence on any other matter. Thus Iain Murray could state that, historically, "a characteristic of an Evangelical was that he put his Evangelical commitment before denominational allegiance and, while he was happy to work in evangelism and conventions with Evangelicals of other denominations, he avoided corporate witness and activity with those who were not of like faith."[24] Murray captures a number of important points here. First, evangelicals have been and should be unabashed in making "evangelical" (rightly understood) our primary Christian identity, since we are about the gospel before anything else. Second, this does not entail abandoning other doctrines such as those that distinguish denominations; it simply recognizes that not all doctrines—even important ones—are foundational, first-level truths. Third, evangelicals do not merely share common beliefs: loving each other as brothers and sisters in Christ, we actively pursue fellowship across denominational lines to make manifest our spiritual unity. Fourth, such fellowship does not require comprehensive agreement on secondary and tertiary issues. Such matters can and should be vigorously and graciously debated by evangelicals in a way that does not question or impair our more fundamental unity in the gospel.

True catholicity does not require a monolithic institution. There will always be denominational differences reflecting differences

---

24 Iain Murray, "Divisive Unity," *The Master's Seminary Journal* 12, no. 2 (Fall 2001): 234.

among evangelicals over matters such as baptism and church polity. But the evangelical spirit seeks to follow the wisdom of J. C. Ryle, who counseled, "Keep the walls of separation as low as possible, and shake hands over them as often as you can."[25] Keeping in mind the ordering of different tiers of doctrine helps us know the level of fellowship we can expect and enjoy with others. With fellow evangelicals, we expect and seek to express the deepest unity of heart and mind, but we don't imagine that means we all could be members of the same denomination or organization. That will seem too abstract to those who prefer a mere external unity, and it can be unacceptably abstract if we never work to *express* our unity in the gospel visibly. Yet it is how we maintain a unity *in the gospel* over a unity found in politics, race, culture, or denomination.

Lowest-Common-Denominator Theology?

There is a caricature of evangelicalism that manages to put many people off. In it, evangelicalism is portrayed as the vacuous and hormonal teenager of Christianity: juvenile, empty-headed, and a slave to every fad. The trouble is, this parody exists not only in the imagination. Much that co-opts the name "evangelical" *is* historically and theologically rootless and therefore shallow and fickle. But doesn't every tradition have a shallow end? Caricatures can be found of every Christian tradition, and it is unfair to judge anything by the worst examples of its kind. The suggestion that such lowest-common-denominator churchmanship is the *logical* final destination for evangelicalism is scurrilous.

---

25 J. C. Ryle, *Charges and Addresses* (Edinburgh: Banner of Truth, 1978), 297.

Evangelicalism is not a slippery slope to theological fluffiness; it is a path of *wisdom* and *proportion*. For evangelicals do not claim that the saving essential truths of the gospel are the only truths that matter, but that the gospel alone is our unifying anchor. We seek to believe and uphold *all* that Scripture teaches. After all, we are people who believe in the supremacy of Scripture, and it is only consistent that we should seek to have a deeply thought-through scriptural view of everything. But we do not believe that every truth is equally important or equally salvific. We are not saved by our knowledge of obscure doctrines. We do not find them the source of our unity. Thus, we hold each matter with the weighting Scripture gives, neither diminishing its primary truths nor elevating the others.

Shallowness is not the natural fruit of evangelicalism, but a perversion. The truer mark of the evangelical is *discernment*. Holding firm to the gospel, and holding it supreme, we reject all that opposes or presumes to rival it—and that must include the tribalism that elevates personalities, culture, politics, or any other issue to the level of the gospel. For evangelicals seek, before all things, to be people of the gospel, not people of a sect.

6

Gospel Integrity

AT THE END OF THIS BOOK, I'm forced to ask the question: Is evangelicalism today truly evangelical? One 2020 survey found that 30 percent of American "evangelicals" believe that Jesus is not God; 65 percent believe he is instead the first being created by God; 46 percent believe the Holy Spirit is a force, not a person; and in any case, 23 percent feel that belief is a matter of opinion, not objective truth.[1] One might quibble with such statistics, but there can be doubt that large numbers of self-confessed "evangelicals" in the United States are not robustly evangelical in their beliefs.

Those figures will undoubtedly be lower in other parts of the world where "evangelicalism" is less a part of the culture. But even then, the picture is often far from rosy. In country after country, we hear stories of abusive and self-serving evangelical leaders. And they are surely only the more noticeable symptoms of a deeper

1 The State of Theology (website), accessed April 22, 2021, https://thestateoftheology.com/.

malaise. The same spiritual emptiness that causes dramatic and high-profile falls from grace also stifles heartfelt worship in the pew. It leeches courage in the face of opposition. It opens the gates to charlatans who offer counterfeit gospels. It encourages a defensive maintenance mode of church management and a hollow, functional approach to the Christian life. In other words, even where evangelicals still confess the faith of the gospel, they can be unworthy of the name.

So no, evangelicalism today is not truly or fully evangelical. At worst, when a non-Trinitarian is described as "evangelical," it is hard to know what is meant by the word. No wonder many distance themselves from it. At best, all evangelicals fail. None are completely faithful as people of the gospel.

We should not seek to excuse ourselves or gloss over the problems. It runs against the very grain of the gospel we cherish for us to indulge in self-justification. Instead, the evangelical way is not to condone or to flee but to repent and to reform. For evangelicalism, being a gospel movement, is and always has been a renewal movement: we seek to renew ourselves and the church around the gospel (and never vice versa). It is a reformation movement, about adhering ever closer to the gospel in thought, word, and deed. On that reformation hangs the future of evangelicalism.

The Apostolic Challenge

At the end of the first chapter of his letter to the Philippians, Paul issues an *evangelical* call to constant reformation. He writes of "the gospel of Christ" and "the faith of the gospel," urging his readers to live as people of the gospel.

Only let your manner of life be worthy of the gospel of Christ, so that whether I come and see you or am absent, I may hear of you that you are standing firm in one spirit, with one mind striving side by side for the faith of the gospel. (Phil. 1:27)

Paul wrote as a prisoner, torn between life and death. For himself, he would "depart and be with Christ, for that is far better" (v. 23), and yet he knew "to remain in the flesh is more necessary on your account" (v. 24). But whether he lived or died, his ultimate concern was not what might happen to him but what will happen to the gospel. From that concern erupts a passionate double plea: (1) to live worthy of the gospel of Christ and (2) to stand firm in one spirit, with one mind striving side by side for the faith of the gospel. It is a summons of apostolic authority to all the renewal we need.

Live Worthy of the Gospel

"Evangelical identity is, in the end, a matter of evangelical integrity," writes Albert Mohler.[2] Without such integrity, the world will see no more than a travesty of the gospel and a distortion of what it means to live in its light. Thus, if evangelicalism is to have a future worthy of the name, we who would be people of the gospel must cultivate an integrity to the gospel, and on more than paper. Mere subscription to a formula is not enough.

But what does evangelical integrity look like? The subject Paul turns to (with a connecting "So") in Philippians 2:1–11, having just called them to live worthy of the gospel, is surely indicative:

2   R. Albert Mohler Jr., "Confessional Evangelicalism," in *Four Views on the Spectrum of Evangelicalism*, ed. Andrew David Naselli and Collin Hansen (Grand Rapids, MI: Zondervan, 2011), 96.

So if there is any encouragement in Christ, any comfort from love, any participation in the Spirit, any affection and sympathy, complete my joy by being of the same mind, having the same love, being in full accord and of one mind. Do nothing from selfish ambition or conceit, but in humility count others more significant than yourselves. Let each of you look not only to his own interests, but also to the interests of others. Have this mind among yourselves, which is yours in Christ Jesus, who, though he was in the form of God, did not count equality with God a thing to be grasped, but emptied himself, by taking the form of a servant, being born in the likeness of men. And being found in human form, he humbled himself by becoming obedient to the point of death, even death on a cross. Therefore God has highly exalted him and bestowed on him the name that is above every name, so that at the name of Jesus every knee should bow, in heaven and on earth and under the earth, and every tongue confess that Jesus Christ is Lord, to the glory of God the Father.

I suggest that at the heart of evangelical integrity is humility. That might seem a laughable claim amid all the empire-building and hubris that has blackened the name of evangelicalism. And there is something about evangelicalism that can make it a fertile soil for pride. Evangelicals are people of the word, and so learning is in the blood. Yet learning so commonly fosters arrogance. Then there is that confidence that we have the truth, an assurance that can buckle into a pharisaical censoriousness that makes many seek refuge elsewhere. John Stott maintained that "the supreme quality which the evangelical faith engenders (or should do) is humility."

And yet, he admitted, "Evangelical people are often regarded as proud, vain, arrogant and cocksure."[3]

What effect should the gospel have on us, though? "He must increase, but I must decrease" (John 3:30). For in the gospel is revealed the glory of the living, triune God, and in his light we creatures and sinners are exposed for the little wretches we are. The more we see of the gospel, the more the three persons of the Trinity (and their work of revelation, redemption, and regeneration) are glorified, and so the more we diminish. Through the gospel, we come to realize that without God's revelation, we are left groping in the darkness of ignorance. Without the redemption of the Son, we are utterly lost in our guilt and alienation from God. Without the Spirit's work of regeneration, we are helplessly mired in our sin. In the gospel, God is exalted, and we delight to be abased before him. And only then, when he is lifted up, are people drawn to him (John 12:32).

Times of reformation and renewal in the church have always been marked by this perspective. A fresh sight of the glory and grace of God awakens people both to who he is and to who they are. Unlike how they once thought, they realize that he is great, glorious, and beautiful in his holiness—and they are not. At the sounding of the gospel and the lifting up of Christ, they are like Isaiah, whose vision of the Lord in glory, high and lifted up, caused him to cry "Woe is me! For I am lost; for I am a man of unclean lips, and I dwell in the midst of a people of unclean lips; for my eyes have seen the King, the LORD of hosts!" (Isa. 6:5). Alternative gospels, where sin is a small problem and so Christ a small savior (or assistant), never have the same effect.

---

3   John Stott, *Evangelical Truth: A Personal Plea for Unity* (Leicester: IVP, 1999), 147.

That sight of God in his glory—now by faith, but one day face to face—is what we are made for. It is through that wonderful sight that we are transformed into his image and become more fully alive and human (2 Cor. 3:18). The humility we learn at the foot of the gospel, glorying in Christ and not ourselves, therefore turns out to be the wellspring of all evangelical health. When our eyes are opened to the love of God for us sinners, we let slip our masks. Condemned as sinners yet justified, we can begin to be honest about ourselves. Loved despite our unloveliness, we begin to love. Given peace with God, we begin to know an inner peace and joy. Shown the magnificence of God above all things, we become more resilient, trembling in wonder at God, and not man.

This was the evangelical transformation Martin Luther experienced through the gospel. Luther often described himself as an anxious young man, being so wrapped up in himself that everything frightened him. Even the sound of a leaf blown in the wind would make him flee (see Lev. 26:36). That changed through his encounter with the gospel of Christ, as Roland Bainton recounts in the splendid final words of his biography:

The God of Luther, as of Moses, was the God who inhabits the storm clouds and rides on the wings of the wind. At his nod the earth trembles, and the people before him are as a drop in the bucket. He is a God of majesty and power, inscrutable, terrifying, devastating, and consuming in his anger. Yet the All Terrible is the All Merciful too. "Like as a father pitieth his children, so the Lord . . ." But how shall we know this? In Christ, only in Christ. In the Lord of life, born in the squalor of a cow stall and dying as a malefactor under the desertion and the derision of men, crying unto God and receiving for answer only the trembling of the earth and the blinding of the sun, even by God forsaken, and in that hour taking to himself and annihilating our iniquity, trampling down the hosts of hell and disclosing within the wrath of the All Terrible the love that will not let us go.[4]

This, concludes Bainton, was the effect:

No longer did Luther tremble at the rustling of a wind-blown leaf, and instead of calling upon St. Anne he declared himself able to laugh at thunder and jagged bolts from out the storm. This was what enabled him to utter such words as these: "Here I stand. I cannot do otherwise. God help me. Amen."[5]

The evangelical humility Luther found before the majesty and mercy of God was not gloomy or timid, forlorn or feeble. It was full-throttled, joyous, and valiant.

That is the stamp of the humility that is found in the gospel, and the look of evangelical integrity. It is the bearing of one refreshed by the gospel. Captivated by the magnificence of God, such evangelicals will not be so drawn to man-centered therapeutic religion. Under the radiance of his glory, they will not want to establish their own little empires. Their tiny achievements will seem petty, their feuds and personal agendas odious. He will loom large, making them bold to please God and not men. They will

---

4 Roland H. Bainton, *Here I Stand: A Life of Martin Luther* (Nashville, TN: Abingdon, 1950), 385–86.

5 Bainton, *Here I Stand*, 386.

not dither or stammer with the gospel. But aware of their own redemption they will share his own meekness and gentleness, not breaking a bruised reed. They will be quick to serve, quick to bless, quick to repent, and quick to laugh at themselves, for their glory is not themselves but Christ. This is the integrity found through the lifting up of Christ in his gospel.

Evangelicalism is in need of much healing, but it needs no other cure than the gospel itself. It needs only integrity.

Strive Side by Side for the Gospel

That integrity is the essential prerequisite for answering the second part of Paul's plea in Philippians 1:27, that Christians stand firm in one spirit, with one mind striving side by side for the faith of the gospel. Note Paul's logic:

> Only let your manner of life be worthy of the gospel of Christ, *so that* whether I come and see you or am absent, I may hear of you that you are standing firm in one spirit, with one mind striving side by side for the faith of the gospel. (Phil. 1:27)

Paul wants to see unity in the gospel, or faithfulness together, but true unity and faithfulness are manifestations of gospel integrity. They will be achieved only by the working of the gospel, when the Son of Man is lifted up, drawing people together to himself.

Paul's concern for Christian unity is a golden thread running through his letter to the Philippians. He wants them to be

> of the same mind, having the same love, being in full accord and of one mind. Do nothing from selfish ambition or conceit,

but in humility count others more significant than yourselves. Let each of you look not only to his own interests, but also to the interests of others. (Phil. 2:2–4)

The Puritan Richard Sibbes wrote that Paul is in effect saying, "Unless you will disclaim all consolation in Christ, &c., labour to maintain the unity of the Spirit in the bond of peace. What a joyful spectacle is this to Satan and his faction, to see those that are separated from the world fall in pieces among themselves! Our discord is our enemy's melody."[6] Discord is devilish; unity is a mark of gospel health. People of the gospel must therefore strive to stand firm in one spirit together.

Yet no call to unity, however stirring, will itself achieve unity. Some deeper work in us is needed. Our devilish pride must be dealt with before our devilish discord disappears. It is why Paul calls the Philippians to have the mindset of Christ, that essential humility the gospel gives. Humility is the only soil in which true unity can grow. Only when Christ is more precious to us than our own reputations will we give up our petty rivalries and personal agendas. Only when his glory eclipses all else will we live for his cause and no other. The unity we need will be the fruit of a fresh humbling before the glory of Christ.

The unity Paul desires does not mean agreement in every detail. Nor is it a unity at any price. It is certainly not a unity at the cost of gospel clarity. It is striving side by side *for the faith of the gospel.* It is faithfulness *together.* As Paul writes, it is also clear that this faithfulness he longs to see in Christians involves resilience. For

6 Richard Sibbes, *The Complete Works of Richard Sibbes,* ed. Alexander Balloch Grosart, vol. 1 (Edinburgh: James Nichol, 1862), 76.

when we strive side by side for the gospel, we will face opposition. We should expect to suffer. We should expect to be maligned and smeared, perhaps imprisoned, maybe even killed. Thus, when he calls us to strive "side by side for the faith of the gospel" (Phil. 1:27), he immediately adds

> and not frightened in anything by your opponents. This is a clear sign to them of their destruction, but of your salvation, and that from God. For it has been granted to you that for the sake of Christ you should not only believe in him but also suffer for his sake, engaged in the same conflict that you saw I had and now hear that I still have. (Phil. 1:28–30)

This, surely, is the desire of every healthy evangelical, to see people of the gospel united in their stand for the things of the gospel. To see an end to *both* the fractious tribalism that elevates other issues to the level of the gospel *and* the treachery that gives up the essential truths of the faith. To see evangelicals standing together on the supremacy and trustworthiness of God's revelation, heralding the one true God, the completeness and sufficiency of Christ's redemption, and the necessity and importance of the Spirit's regeneration.

Where does such united, sturdy faithfulness come from? Paul seems clear: "if there is any encouragement in Christ, any comfort from love, any participation in the Spirit" (Phil. 2:1). Willingness to be faithful to the gospel, even to the point of suffering for the gospel, can come only from the gospel itself. It is in Christ that we find courage and comfort. It is when he is exalted and glorious to us that we are prepared to follow him through trials and stand for him against all opposition. In other words, we will see more united loyalty to the gospel when we have a fresher, deeper clarity in the gospel. That is the great need of the hour.

While we are considering our unity in the gospel, it is worth reflecting on the criticism that evangelicals do not stand in unity with the historic church down the centuries. I have argued that that is unfair: evangelicalism is historic, uneccentric, catholic Christianity. However, modern evangelicalism has often displayed an unevangelical individualism that has failed to care about our unity in the gospel with the creeds or with great theologians like Athanasius, Luther, and Edwards. It is not that we should ever replace Scripture with them as our supreme authority. Never. But we would be decidedly foolish to ignore them and fail to heed their wisdom. Without their insights into Scripture ringing in our ears, we will far more easily be swayed by our culture, "blissfully unaware of how faddish our beliefs are."[7] Without a keen awareness of where the church has always stood, the mood of our age—and how we might succumb to it—will be far harder to see. "If we ignore what the bulk of the church has said down through history, then we act as schismatically as if we ignored the church on earth today."[8] True unity in the gospel must include unity with evangelical thought down through history. Thus, C. S. Lewis— while no card-carrying evangelical himself—wisely counseled,

> It is a good rule, after reading a new book, never to allow yourself another new one till you have read an old one in between. If that is too much for you, you should at least read

---

7 Michael Reeves, *Theologians You Should Know: An Introduction: From the Apostolic Fathers to the 21st Century* (Wheaton, IL: Crossway, 2016), 14.

8 Reeves, *Theologians You Should Know*, 15.

one old one to every three new ones. . . . Not, of course, that there is any magic about the past. People were no cleverer then than they are now; they made as many mistakes as we. But not the *same* mistakes. They will not flatter us in the errors we are already committing; and their own errors, being now open and palpable, will not endanger us. Two heads are better than one, not because either is infallible, but because they are unlikely to go wrong in the same direction. To be sure, the books of the future would be just as good a corrective as the books of the past, but unfortunately we cannot get at them.[9]

Diagnosing Ourselves

It is all too easy to deceive ourselves here. If we fail to be clear about which truths are essential to the gospel, we can speak vaguely of the "the gospel" and vainly imagine we are proclaiming and believing it faithfully. Or we can assume the gospel, and take it that brief references to it are all that are needed, as if everyone in our church has been taught well already and they need no more. We can be reactive, driven more by fads, culture, or threats against the gospel than by the gospel itself (witness evangelical anti-intellectual biblicism). Preachers can imagine that they teach with a right biblical balance simply because they always expound Scripture, not seeing that theology and personality will dispose them to notice and pounce on certain themes while they fail to see others. Martyn Lloyd-Jones once said,

9 C. S. Lewis, introduction to Athanasius, *On the Incarnation* (repr., Crestwood, NY: SVS, 1998), 4–5.

I have discovered over the years that subtraction from the truth is something that members of churches are very, very slow to observe. I have almost come to the conclusion that the acid test to apply, to know whether a preacher is evangelical or not, is this: observe what he does not say! So often I have found that people have listened to a man and been carried away by him, and thought everything was wonderful, for the reason that he said nothing wrong, and they were quite right in their observation. The man had said nothing wrong, but the point was that he had not said certain things that an evangelical always must say; he had left them out.[10]

Just as dangerous as that subtraction from the gospel is adding to the gospel. And that too can often be hard to notice or pin down. We can elevate a political agenda or a cultural assumption to the place of primacy only the gospel should have, and that idolatry can be unobserved by all around us simply because they share our tribal assumptions.

To be faithfully evangelical is to teach all that Scripture teaches with Scripture's own emphases and Scripture's own tone. We cannot have a lopsided or truncated faithfulness. So is there a way to apply Lloyd-Jones's acid test to ourselves? To diagnose our faithfulness? If we teach others, is there a health check we can use to protect us from hobbyhorses and gospel reduction, ensuring we give our people a balanced and fully evangelical theological diet?

The following diagram puts together all the theological essentials we have seen. It is not a comprehensive systematic theology!

---

10   D. M. Lloyd-Jones, *What Is an Evangelical?* (Edinburgh: Banner of Truth, 1992), 39.

Evangelicals hold to *all* that Scripture teaches, whereas this simply seeks to lay out the first-tier issues of the gospel. These are not our only concerns; rather, as J. C. Ryle put it, it is

> the *position* which we assign to these points, which is one of the grand characteristics of Evangelical theology. We say boldly that they are first, foremost, chief, and principal things in Christianity, and that want of attention to their position mars and spoils the teaching of many well-meaning Churchmen.[11]

Because doctrines never stand alone, they are all interconnected. Each one involves other doctrines. For example, the very notion of redemption assumes God's good act of creation and its marring in the fall. Equally, it is impossible to teach the new birth faithfully without showing our helplessness in sin and so our *need* for a new birth. And while all are primary truths of the gospel, it is not so simple that we treat them all exactly the same. Scripture, for example, is not an end in itself, but testifies to Christ.

With those caveats in place, look at the diagram and ask yourself:

- Are there truths here that you have unwittingly sidelined?
- If you teach others, which of these truths have you not merely referenced or implied but *taught and unfolded* in the last three years?

11 J. C. Ryle, *Knots Untied* (London: Chas. J. Thynne, 1900), 8.

- Are there secondary, cultural, or political issues you have added to the circle?
- And because consistent evangelicals must *apply* their theology, are there truths here that have not affected your character and life and ministry? Which have been soft-pedalled? Which have gone against the grain, been resisted, or only gone skin-deep?

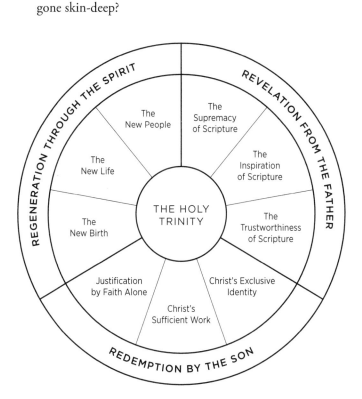

What's in a Name?

I am not interested, primarily, in the label *evangelical*. I want people of the gospel to live and die with integrity as people of the gospel. Yet the labels we use and the identities we adopt do shape perceptions, and so we must ask: What of the name? Is it too muddied or too vague to be salvageable?

Certainly, we need to be judicious in our use of the word *evangelical*. The word has acquired different nuances in different parts of the world, and we need to be wise and contextually sensitive to misunderstandings. In some places, for example, for a church to have the word in its name could give a wrong impression.

My suspicion, though, is that the greater danger lies in the opposite direction: that we too blithely abandon the label as if it were entirely unimportant. When difficulties come, it is easier in the short term to jettison a dirtied label, thinking that another will do as well. The trouble is, the next name we adopt can wear thin very quickly—more quickly, in fact, given the new one's lack of pedigree. And then, when we rebrand ourselves every ten years, the idea that we might represent the historic, catholic faith becomes laughable.

The word *evangelical* has centuries of pedigree for a good reason. It may have lost some of its value *in some places*, but that can be regained through reinvestment. And where else can we people of the gospel go? There really is no acceptable and viable alternative with anything like the historical weight or the descriptive simplicity. As Albert Mohler has said, "Attempts have been made to replace the term *evangelical* with something more useful, but such efforts have met with little success. The reason for this is quite simple: the word really does accomplish what it sets out to do. The word identifies those who find their primary identity as a gospel people."[12]

---

12 Mohler, "Confessional Evangelicalism," 69.

Names do matter. However, the future for evangelicals does not depend on what we are called. Evangelicalism will be strong wherever believers stand shoulder to shoulder contending for the faith that was once and for all delivered to the saints. It will thrive where the people of the gospel have integrity to the gospel.

Appendix 1

Can Evangelicalism Be Defined?

CAN EVANGELICALISM BE DEFINED, or is it so flimsy and malleable that it constantly succumbs to its context, shapeshifting according to when and where it is? Such was D. G. Hart's argument. "Evangelicalism," he wrote, "needs to be relinquished as a religious identity because it does not exist. In fact, it is the wax nose of twentieth-century American Protestantism."[1] (Imagine how strange that sounds to non-American evangelicals.) But Hart is not alone; consider, for example, the quip that an evangelical is just someone who likes Billy Graham. Or take the case of Pope Francis. Shortly after his elevation to the papacy, the media dubbed him the "evangelical pope" because of his apparent Christ-centeredness.[2] Some saw this as proof

---

1 D. G. Hart, *Deconstructing Evangelicalism* (Grand Rapids, MI: Baker, 2004), 16. For a response, see Timothy Larsen, "D. G. Hart, *Deconstructing Evangelicalism: Conservative Protestantism in the Age of Billy Graham*," *The Journal of Religion* 85, no. 1 (January 2005): 120–21.

2 Jennifer Leclaire, "Evangelist Luis Palau Has Laid Hands on Pope Francis," *Charisma News*, March 21, 2013, https://www.charismanews.com/; George Weigle,

that evangelicalism had finally lost all its boundaries, if even the pope could be conscripted into its ranks.

But surely that is unfair. Labeling Pope Francis the "evangelical pope" says nothing more than that the pope was perceived by the media to be leaning in a particular—and *recognizably evangelical*—theological direction. (Of course, whether he was actually leaning toward a more evangelical theology is quite another question.) The Pope Francis example seems more indicative of a widespread confirmation bias: a desire among those disaffected by evangelicalism to look for any proof of the inherent shapelessness of evangelicalism.

"I know what constituted an Evangelical in former times," wrote Lord Shaftesbury in the late nineteenth century; "I have no clear notion what constitutes one now."[3] Written two centuries ago, that could be taken to imply the constancy of confusion over what defines an evangelical. What Shaftesbury meant, though, was simply that confusion had come in where once there had been clarity. And so it is today: in America, in Europe, and elsewhere, there is widespread confusion over what it is to be evangelical and widespread misappropriation of the word. For historical reasons, for example, *evangelische* in German (and *evangelisk* in Swedish) connotes Lutheran, whether liberal or conservative. But none of that confusion means that clarity is impossible to come by. Nor should misuse stop use.

The most common "definition" of evangelicalism found today—and the one that has become the benchmark of all discussions of the subject—is David Bebbington's quadrilateral. There are, he wrote,

"The Christ-Centered Pope," *National Review*, September 20, 2013, https://www.nationalreview.com/.

3   E. Hodder, *The Life and Work of the Seventh Earl of Shaftesbury, K. G.* (London, 1888), 738.

four qualities that have been the special marks of Evangelical religion: *conversionism*, the belief that lives need to be changed; *activism*, the expression of the gospel in effort; *biblicism*, a particular regard for the Bible; and what may be called *cruci-centrism*, a stress on the sacrifice of Christ on the cross.[4]

It may sound so esoteric that few evangelicals would quickly recognize it as theirs, but it does rightly show, as Bebbington wanted, that evangelicalism has "a common core that has remained remarkably constant down the centuries."[5] In fact, that seems to have been Bebbington's main aim: he was setting out, as a historian, to trace common characteristics or family resemblances. He did *not* mean for his quadrilateral to become a "definition" of evangelicalism. Yet it has quickly been *received* as a definition, and *as a definition* it is problematic. For one thing, when read as a comprehensive definition, it makes evangelicalism look sectarian in its choice of these apparently random emphases and its omission of such central doctrines as the Trinity and the person of Christ. When read as a definition, it is also unhelpfully vague. For what pre-Reformation pope would be excluded? The meaning of "lives being changed," "the gospel in effort," "a particular regard for the Bible," and "a stress on the sacrifice of Christ" are so open that many Roman Catholics—even Jehovah's Witnesses—could happily so identify as "evangelical." Indeed, they have.[6]

---

4   D. W. Bebbington, *Evangelicalism in Modern Britain: A History from the 1730s to the 1980s* (London: Unwin Hyman, 1989), 3.

5   Bebbington, *Evangelicalism in Modern Britain*, 4.

6   Mark A. Noll and Carolyn Nystrom, *Is the Reformation Over? An Evangelical Assessment of Contemporary Roman Catholicism* (Grand Rapids, MI: Baker; Milton Keynes: Paternoster, 2005), 12–13, 23.

Perhaps the real problem with taking Bebbington's quadrilateral as a definition, though, is that it gives a historian's *descriptive* analysis. That is, it seeks to describe what you see on the ground among those who call themselves evangelical. Now that is quite right for a historian trying to understand the historical characteristics of a tradition, but we should not *define* a Christian tradition—*any* Christian tradition—like that. We do not, for example, get our understanding of what it means to be Reformed simply by looking around at everything that calls itself Reformed. But we have done so with evangelicalism, and that attempt to define evangelicalism sociologically is precisely the problem at the heart of the evangelical identity crisis today.[7] If "evangelicalism" is merely a sociological category and means nothing more than the common traits of all who wear the label, of course evangelicalism will look a shallow thing. If "evangelical" theology is stretched to fit all that, then it is the product not of historic and biblical doctrines but of whatever theology is currently doing the rounds. In that case,

---

7   In the United States, for example, "evangelicalism" is read by many as a political, cultural, or racial category such that nominal, unregenerate Americans claim the designation of *evangelical* while either not following Christ at all or allowing political tribalism to upstage gospel fidelity. As a British, self-confessed evangelical, it is hard to take in how politically charged the word *evangelicalism* feels in America. For it is just not so on the British side of the pond (or in Australia, Europe, Africa, South America, or South Korea). Outside the US, evangelicals are politically concerned to be sure: we know our theology has political consequences. But we are not a political or racial block. However, while America has unparalleled global influence, it seems odd that the global majority must dance to the tune of a recent American anomaly. There are, after all, many millions more evangelicals outside North America than inside. In fact, there are more in Nigeria and Brazil alone. To judge by percentage of population, the heartlands of evangelicalism today are not the United States or the UK, but South Korea and Kenya. Evangelicalism is a very long way from being an exclusively American reality: American controversies should not be held to define it.

"evangelicalism" *must be* vacuous and faddish. Defining evangelicalism sociologically is a good way to help it sleepwalk into what Francis Schaeffer called "the great evangelical disaster—the failure of the evangelical world to stand for truth as truth. There is," he wrote, "only one word for this—namely accommodation: the evangelical church has accommodated to the world spirit of the age."[8]

Evangelicalism must be defined theologically, by the evangel. A good number of evangelical leaders have made careful attempts to do so, defining evangelicalism theologically, and the harmony of their voices is striking.[9] Some have already been mentioned in this book, but here are three relatively recent definitions laid out in full for comparison.

George Marsden argued that evangelicals are those who hold to:

1. the Reformation doctrine of the final authority of Scripture;
2. the real, historical character of God's saving work recorded in Scripture;
3. eternal salvation only through personal trust in Christ;
4. the importance of evangelism and missions; and
5. the importance of a spiritually transformed life.[10]

Marsden's definition is noticeably similar to J. I. Packer's, demonstrating the level of consensus about evangelicalism among

---

8   Francis Schaeffer, *The Great Evangelical Disaster* (Wheaton, IL: Crossway, 1984), 37.

9   See also J. I. Packer and Thomas Oden, *One Faith: The Evangelical Consensus* (Downers Grove, IL: InterVarsity Press, 2004).

10   George M. Marsden, ed., *Evangelicalism and Modern America* (Grand Rapids, MI: Eerdmans, 1984), ix–x.

evangelical theologians. Packer once listed the six marks of evangelical faith as follows:

1. The supremacy of Holy Scripture
2. The majesty of Jesus Christ
3. The lordship of the Holy Spirit
4. The necessity of conversion
5. The priority of evangelism
6. The importance of fellowship[11]

Elsewhere, he wrote of another "distinguishing mark of the worldwide evangelical fraternity":

1. Penal Substitutionary Atonement[12]

It may at first seem that these seven marks are an unwarranted leap away from the simplicity of having but a material principle (the gospel) and a formal principle (the truth and supremacy of the Scriptures). But there is something compelling about Packer's list: the first three are clearly theological, the next three the practical outworkings of that theology (and, one might say, the seventh mark is really just an elaboration of the second). They show that the *practical* concerns of evangelicalism flow from *theological* convictions. In other words, evangelicals act, not out of cultural or political leanings, but out of theological, biblical convictions.

---

11 J. I. Packer, *The Evangelical Anglican Identity Problem: An Analysis* (Oxford: Latimer House, 1978), 20–23.
12 J. I. Packer, "What Did the Cross Achieve? The Logic of Penal Substitution," *Tyndale Bulletin*, 25 (1974): 3.

More importantly, Packer's first three theological marks are *Trinitarian*. They show that evangelicals do not detach the gospel from the God of the gospel.

John Stott believed that this Trinitarian, theology-led description of evangelicalism could be made even clearer and simpler. He therefore amended Packer's list, bringing everything—the theological and the practical—under three essential marks:

1. Bible: the revelation of God the Father
2. Cross: the redemption of God the Son
3. Spirit: the ministry of God the Spirit[13]

Here, the evangelical concerns for conversion, evangelism, and fellowship (also flagged by Marsden) are clearly made, not additions to the theology, but an extension and application of it. And it is not that Stott crassly shoehorned everything into three simply for the look of being Trinitarian. He saw that evangelicals want to be clear about which God they worship (so as not to be confused with groups such as the Jehovah's Witnesses). They also want to be clear that their theology derives from Scripture. And lastly, they actually need to be clear on *two* things about the gospel: the unique, redemptive work of Christ and the ongoing, regenerative work of the Spirit.

---

13 John Stott, *Evangelical Truth: A Personal Plea for Unity* (Leicester: IVP, 1999), 28, 103.

Appendix 2

Does Evangelicalism Have a History?

"I WANT TO ARGUE," said John Stott, "that the Evangelical Faith is nothing other than the historic Christian faith: original, biblical, apostolic Christianity."[1] Rather than being a backwater off the mainstream of Christianity, it *is* the original mainstream, he argued: the Christianity of the apostles, the Apostles' Creed, and the Nicene Creed. J. I. Packer similarly described evangelicalism as "in principle nothing but Christianity itself. The critics call it a new heresy. We shall give reasons for regarding it as the oldest orthodoxy. . . . A consistent Evangelicalism is the truest catholicity."[2] Both were echoing J. C. Ryle, who asserted "that a religion to be really 'Evangelical' and really good, must be the Gospel, the whole Gospel, and nothing but the Gospel, as Christ prescribed it

---

1 Michael Reeves and John Stott, *The Reformation: What You Need to Know and Why* (Peabody, MA: Hendrickson, 2017), 31.
2 J. I. Packer, *"Fundamentalism" and the Word of God* (Leicester: Inter-Varsity Fellowship, 1958), 22.

and expounded it to the Apostles."[3] And if evangelicalism really is "mere Christianity," how could it be anything but the oldest orthodoxy of the apostles?

Yet in most modern discussions of evangelicalism, it is presented as a quite recent phenomenon: perhaps as a twentieth-century tribe distinguished from fundamentalism, or as the legacy of the eighteenth-century revivalists. Which all helps feed the sneaking suspicion that John Henry Newman was right: "To be deep in history is to cease to be a Protestant."[4] And if evangelicalism is no more than a historical novelty, it has little right to command long-term allegiance. When it gets dirty, something so cheap can be thrown out without a care.

A good part of the problem comes from how historians like to track evangelicalism through use of the word *evangelical*. Approached like this, we see some evangelicals before the Reformation (like John Wycliffe, the "*doctor evangelicus*"). But the real rise of evangelicalism, on this way of thinking, would start in the sixteenth century when early Reformers, before they were described as Protestant or Lutheran or Calvinist, were referred to as "Evaungelicalles."[5] Usage then grows through the Puritan era until in the eighteenth century we see it used widely both of and by men like George Whitefield, the Wesleys, Jonathan Edwards, and Charles Simeon. The following century, in 1846, the World Evangelical Alliance was founded, and evangelicalism began to take on its modern look, further defined in

3   J. C. Ryle, *Knots Untied* (London: Chas. J. Thynne, 1900), 19.

4   J. H. Newman, *Essay on the Development of Christian Doctrine* (London: Tooley, 1845), 8.

5   Peter Marshall, "Evangelical conversion in the reign of Henry VIII," in *The Beginnings of English Protestantism*, ed. Peter Marshall and Alec Ryrie (Cambridge: Cambridge University Press, 2002), 14–37.

the United States by the twentieth-century National Association of Evangelicals. When looked at like this, it is all too easy to emphasize the differences from age to age, giving the impression of an infinite elasticity to the term *evangelicalism*. Thus, where *evangelical* in the sixteenth century meant anti-Catholic, in the eighteenth century it meant antiformalist, and in the nineteenth century antiliberal. Worse, we are told, before about 1800, *evangelical* was normally an adjective, not a noun, making *evangelical* even less definable.

Historical use of the word *evangelical* does in fact point to a real continuity that existed down the centuries. But without pressing deeper, the strength of that continuity can be missed. Merely looking at historical use of the word will fail to appreciate how indebted George Whitefield (1714–1770) was to Henry Scougal (1650–1678); William Grimshaw (1708–1763) was to John Owen (1616–1683); Charles Spurgeon (1834–1892) was to the Puritans; or Calvin (1509–1564) was to Augustine (354–430). Moreover, the very fact that *evangelical* has tended to be an adjective tells us more than any listing of where the label has been applied down the centuries. It shows us that the roots of evangelicalism go deeper than the usage of the name. To be evangelical means to be faithful to the gospel. That, of course, will look different according to the issues and the challenges of the day. For example, to be faithful to the gospel may look a little different in a Roman Catholic context where justification by faith alone is denied than in a liberal one where the truthfulness of Scripture is denied. In the Roman Catholic context, more apologetic work will be needed for justification; in a liberal context, more will be needed for the reliability of Scripture. The difference between the two does not imply rootlessness but faithfulness.

This was just how those "early" evangelicals, the Reformers, understood what it meant to be evangelical. Take, for example, how the Second Helvetic Confession uses the word: "The preaching and writings of the apostles, in which the apostles explain for us how the Son was given to us by the Father, and in him everything that has to do with life and salvation, is also rightly called evangelical doctrine."[6] In their desire to be evangelical, the Reformers were not seeking to conform to any tradition or party. Nor did they believe they were in any way innovative. "We are not teaching anything novel," wrote Luther, "we are repeating and confirming old doctrines."[7] In fact, when charged with innovation by the Roman Catholic church, John Calvin replied,

> Our agreement with antiquity is far closer than yours, but that all we have attempted has been to renew that ancient form of the Church, which, at first sullied and distorted by illiterate men of indifferent character, was afterwards flagitiously mangled and almost destroyed by the Roman Pontiff and his faction.[8]

Seeing this, Kenneth J. Stewart, in his book *In Search of Ancient Roots*, was able to lay out the case that the evangelical impulse in Christianity has been with us since the apostles.[9] And while *every*

---

6 Second Helvetic Confession, chap. 13, Christian Classics Ethereal Library (website), accessed September 15, 2021, https://www.ccel.org/.

7 Martin Luther, *Lectures on Galatians, 1535, Chapters 1–4*, vol. 26 of *Luther's Works*, ed. Jaroslav Jan Pelikan, Hilton C. Oswald, and Helmut T. Lehmann (Philadelphia, PA: Fortress, 1999), 39.

8 John Calvin, "Reply to Sadoleto," in John Calvin and Jacopo Sadoleto, *A Reformation Debate*, ed. John C. Olin (Grand Rapids, MI: Baker, 1966), 62.

9 Kenneth J. Stewart, *In Search of Ancient Roots: The Christian Past and the Evangelical Identity Crisis* (London: Apollos, 2017).

Christian tradition has altered in some respect down through the centuries, what marks out true evangelicalism is that it constantly reforms, not to conform to each new era (as others might), but to be faithful to the gospel amid the particular challenges each one presents.

General Index

Abraham, 60
abuse, 105
Adam, 37, 49–50, 57
alternative gospels, 109
"Amazing Grace" (Newton), 67
American Protestantism, 123
Amsterdam Declaration (2000), 99
anti-intellectualism, 116
Apostles' Creed, 19, 131
apostolic authority, 26n3, 107, 132, 134
Arminianism, 95
arrogance, 108–9
ascension, 56
Ashley-Cooper, Anthony (Lord Shaftesbury), 124
Athanasius, 26–27, 49–50, 115
atonement, 57, 59–60, 128
Augustine, 27, 38, 68–69, 72, 78–79, 133
authorities, 30–35

Bainton, Roland, 110–11
baptism, 74, 89
Baptists, 99
Barth, Karl, 39
Basil of Caesarea, 62

Bebbington, David, 67, 124–25, 126
biblicism, 33, 43, 116
blurring, 90–96

Calvinists, 95, 132
Calvin, John, 61, 133, 134
Caroline Divines, 80–81
Carson, D. A., 98–99
Catechism of the Catholic Church, 92
catholicity, 27n6, 66–67, 115
Catholic Theological Society of America, 100
Charles I, 80
Chicago Statement on Biblical Inerrancy, 41
Christian identity, 102
Chrysostom, John, 62
church councils, 32
church government, 89
Church of England, 80
Collins, Kenneth, 100
confirmation bias, 124
conversion, 74, 129
conversionism, 67, 75
Corban, 24, 25

Scripture Index

Also Available from Michael Reeves

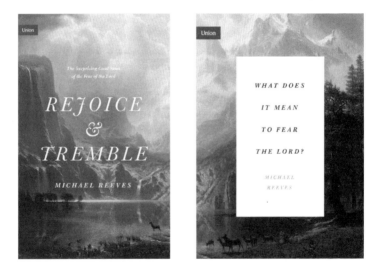